THE STORY OF LANKA

THE STORY OF LANKA

OUTLINES OF THE HISTORY OF CEYLON FROM THE EARLIEST TIMES TO THE COMING OF THE PORTUGUESE

L. E. BLAZE

GYAN

Published by

Gyan Publishing House
5, Ansari Road
Daryaganj, New Delhi-110002
Phone: 011-47034999, 9811692060
E-mail: books@gyanbooks.com

Distribution Network
gyanbooks.com
India, USA, Canada, UK, Australia, France

ISBN : 978-81-212-4067-3 (PB)
First Published, Colombo, 1921

2nd Impression 2020

Printed at: Gyan Press, Delhi.

The Story of Lanka
Author: L. E. Blaze

THE STORY OF LANKA:

Outlines of the History of Ceylon from the earliest times to the coming of the Portuguese.

BY

L. E. BLAZE, B.A.

Second Edition.

The Christian Literature Society for India,
London, Madras and Colombo

1921

CONTENTS

NOTE TO THE SECOND EDITION.

The aim of this book was stated in the Preface to the First Edition of 1914.

"This little book tells the "Story of Lanka" as briefly and simply as I can tell it. I have tried to omit everything that was not essential to a right understanding of the course of events, and have borne in mind always that pupils in the Fifth Standard (where alone, till this year, the History of Ceylon was allowed to be taught) cannot be expected to shew the same interest and intelligence as "children of a larger growth." The aim of the book is to teach History, and any capable teacher should be able to separate the legendary from what is purely historical."

This new edition has been carefully revised and an Index has been added. I have to thank Mr. L. J. Gratiaen, B.A. for helpful suggestions, some of which I hope to use on another occasion; and Mudaliyar Simon De Silva for revising the spelling of proper names. The Mudaliyar insists that the Tamil invasion referred to on page 112 was during the reign of Vikrama Bahu III, and that the Portuguese came to Ceylon during the reign of Vira Parakrama Bahu who preceded Dharma Parakrama Bahu IX. He is probably right; but it seemed better to leave the text as it stands, as much new light is still being thrown on the darkness of the period.

I have also to thank A. R. B. and Mr. C. W. H. Lutersz for willing assistance in the reading of the proofs.

L. E. B.

Kingswood,
Kandy, July, 1921.

THE STORY OF LANKA

I.

THE STORY OF LANKA

MANY, if not all, of us must have learnt by this time something of the *Geography* of Ceylon—that is, about the position of Ceylon with regard to India and other countries, about its size, its people and the work they do, its mountains and rivers, its chief towns and provinces. We have now to learn how this island has come to be in the condition in which we now find it; how it happens that so many races of people—Sinhalese, Tamils, Moors, Malays, Burghers, English, &c.—are here, and how they first came here. We shall learn what each of these races did in Ceylon in former times, and what each race is now doing for the island. We shall learn something about the great kings and great leaders that Ceylon has produced. We shall read of battles and sieges; of victories and defeats; of adventures and escapes; and also of the making of new towns and the beginning of new industries. To study these things is to study the *History* of Ceylon.

In this study we shall find much that will interest us. Stories, for instance, of brave deeds and of great men are always pleasing; and our pleasure must be greater when these stories are about our own land and our own people. But apart from the pleasure, it is useful and even necessary for us to know the history of the land in which we live and to which we belong. When we grow up to be men and women we shall, all of us, have to take our share in making Ceylon a more prosperous country, and the people of Ceylon a happier people. A knowledge of our history will help us by explaining many things that otherwise we shall not understand.

As Ceylon is so near India it is not difficult to suppose that the people who first of all lived in Ceylon were very like the people of Southern India; not indeed like the educated Malabars, Tamils, and others who live there now, but like the uncivilized tribes who live in the hills and jungles of South India, as our Veddas live in the hills and jungles of Uva and the Eastern Province. About three thousand years ago, a prince named Rama is said to have come with a great army from India to Ceylon. He conquered and killed the king of Ceylon and returned to India. This is almost the first story we know about Ceylon—or **Lanka**, as it was then named—though we cannot be sure how much of the story is quite true.

The next story is that of Vijaya who also was an Indian prince Vijaya, with a large number of followers, sailed to Ceylon about five hundred years before the birth of Christ, or about two thousand four hundred years ago He conquered the people whom he found here, and his followers went into different parts of the country and settled down as chiefs and rulers. Their descendants are the people who call themselves **Sinhalese**. The Sinhalese became a great nation. They built large cities, wonderful temples, and immense tanks; they divided the country into provinces, made laws, and kept order among themselves. Buddhism afterwards became their religion, and the kings were so attentive to religious ceremonies that they often neglected to train armies and to build forts to defend the country from the attacks of other nations.

Many of the Sinhalese kings married princesses from South India, and in this way the **Tamils** began to come into Ceylon. In a short time the Tamils tried to get the whole island to themselves, and thus they were constantly at war with the Sinhalese. Sometimes the Tamils won; at other times the Sinhalese succeeded in driving them away. In the end the Tamils were able to settle undisturbed in the northern and eastern parts of the island.

After a thousand and more years of war and peace both nations were disturbed by the unexpected appearance of a Portuguese ship. The **Portuguese** were the people of Portugal, a country in Europe. They were a brave nation who sailed in their own ships into the most distant parts of the world. No other nation had dared to do this before. They had already conquered several towns and districts on the west coast of India, and the ship that came to Ceylon came from Goa, their chief town in India. There were Portuguese settlements in Malacca also, far to the east of Ceylon, and as Colombo and Galle were convenient harbours where their ships might halt on the long voyage between Goa and Malacca, the Portuguese determined to get Ceylon for themselves. Not long after their first visit they came again, and, little by little, conquered those districts of Ceylon which were near the sea, and settled there. The Sinhalese who would not submit to Portuguese rule went to the hill districts round Kandy, where a Sinhalese king still reigned, and where the Portuguese could not easily reach them.

The Portuguese were Roman Catholic Christians and brought their religion with them to Ceylon. They held the coast provinces for about a hundred and twenty-three years and then they were driven out by the **Dutch** (the people of Holland, another country in Europe) who were Protestant Christians. The Dutch wanted to get into their hands the profitable trade which the Portuguese had so long carried on with the East. The Dutch ruled the coast provinces for a hundred and forty years and then had to go away Their descendants in Ceylon are the *Burghers*, a Dutch word, still commonly applied to Dutch people.

The English took Ceylon from the Dutch in the year 1796; that is, they took the coast provinces. The Kandyans of the hill districts were still unconquered and still had their own king and their own laws and customs. It was not till the year 1815 that the English took possession of Kandy, and the whole of Ceylon then came under the rule of a European nation.

II.

RAMA AND SITA

Rama was a brave and honourable prince who lived, about three thousand years ago, in that part of Northern India which is now called Oudh. All the people of Oudh loved him for his courage, his wisdom, and his gentleness towards them. But through his step-mother's jealousy and cunning he was unjustly banished for fourteen years from his father's kingdom.

Rama's bride was the beautiful princess **Sita**, the daughter of a friendly king. So many princes had wished to marry her that a great competition in arms was held, and Sita was to be the bride of the most worthy. Rama won the prize by taking up and bending a huge bow that no other man could even raise from the ground.

With his bride, the beautiful princess Sita, and Lakshmana, his favourite brother, Rama travelled southwards, visiting sacred places in the jungles of Central India, where pious Brahmans used to live far away from the busy and noisy world. Here complaints were often brought to him about a terrible race of demons, called Rakshasas, who had the power of appearing in different shapes when they pleased, and who were giving much trouble to the pious hermits. The two brothers would continually fight the Rakshasas and drive them away. At length Rama came in his wanderings to a pleasant forest on the banks of the river Godaveri, and here the exiles lived happily for some time.

But in this very forest there dwelt a number of Rakshasas, and the report of Rama's doings and of the Princess Sita's beauty, came to the ears of **Ravana**, the ten-necked king of the Rakshasas. Ravana's chief city was Lankapura, in the island of Lanka, as Ceylon was then called, and he made up his mind to carry Sita to Lanka, and there to make her his Queen. He could not do this by force as Sita was too carefully guarded by her husband and his brother; but by a clever trick he at last succeeded. One day there came near Rama's forest dwelling a wonderfully beautiful deer, each of his horns tipped with a bright sapphire, and his skin shining like polished gold. Sita was attracted by the unusual beauty of the deer, and begged Rama to get it for her. Rama was sure that some trick was being played by the Rakshasas, but as Sita wished so much to have the deer, he went after it, leaving Lakshmana in charge of the cottage. The deer, which was really a Rakshasa in disguise, took Rama far away, but when it was at last shot down it imitated

Rama's voice and called aloud for help. The cry was heard in the cottage, and Sita believing that Rama was in danger forced Lakshmana against his will to go to his brother. She was thus left alone, and was easily carried away by the Rakshasa king.

But she knew that Rama would follow to save her, and as the ten-necked demon-king bore her through the air, she dropped her jewels one by one to the ground, so that Rama might know where she was taken. Thus it was he found the way to her, and the king of the vultures, who had tried to save Sita and was wounded to death in doing so, told Rama how Ravana had carried Sita away to Lanka.

Now Lanka was an island in the middle of the ocean, and to get across from India Rama had to get the help of the king of the Monkeys, who was the chief king in South India. This king gave orders to Hanuman, one of the wisest of the Monkey chiefs, and Hanuman boldly but secretly went across to Sita in Lanka with a message from Rama, and brought back news of her ; but so fond of mischief was he that, before leaving Lanka, he set fire to Ravana's city and destroyed a large part of it.

Rama and his new friends then crossed over to Lanka. Millions of Monkeys, and of Bears too, brought stones and trees from the hills and the forests and threw them into the sea. In this way was formed—so the story tells us —the passage now known as Adam's Bridge ; and the armies of Rama soon came before

Lankapura, the golden city of Lanka. It was indeed a glorious city, built among high mountains, and defended by seven walls one within the other,—the first wall being of iron, the next of stone, and the innermost of shining gold. The city had splendid gates, broad and well-kept roads, beautiful temples, palaces, and jewelled courts, and gardens where grew countless trees laden with tempting fruit and with flowers delightful for beauty and fragrance. There were horses and elephants and chariots for use in war; and skilled musicians to please, in times of peace, the demon-king and his multitudes of obedient subjects. Well might Ravana be proud of his royal city.

But the hosts of Rama, though they had only stones and trees for weapons, were too strong for the demon-king, though the demons had arrows, swords, and spears. One after the other, Ravana's best captains were killed, all fighting bravely to the end. One of his brothers left him to join the enemy. Still Ravana would not yield. For ten years Lankapura held out. and then at last Ravana was killed by a charmed arrow which a friendly hand gave Rama, and the city was taken.

The conqueror afterwards returned to India leaving Ravana's brother, who had joined Rama to govern Lanka. This brother is still worshipped in Lanka as the god Vibhisana. And there are places in Ceylon which still remind us of Rama's beautiful princess—places with names like Sitawaka, Sita-kotuwa, Sita-ella.

III.

HOW THE SINHALESE CAME TO LANKA

More than two thousand years ago, there lived in Northern India a king whose name was Sinha-bahu. He was so called because his father was said to have been a *Sinha*, or lion; which means only that the father was a bold, bad man, of lower rank than the princess whom he married; or that he belonged to a different race. In the same way, we must understand that the vultures, monkeys, bears, and demons spoken of before were only tribes of men so named by a prouder race.

The eldest son of Sinha-bahu was prince Vijaya. As Vijaya was to be king when his father died, he should have been a kind and well behaved prince, but unfortunately he was quite the opposite. His evil deeds gave his father much trouble. He got together a company of seven hundred young men as wicked as himself, and with them continually ill-treated the people of the country. The people complained to the king, and more than once the king warned his son that such conduct was dangerous. But Vijaya and his lawless company took no notice of the king's warnings. At last, the people could no longer bear the wickedness of the prince, and coming to the king in large numbers they demanded that

Vijaya should be put to death. The king did not wish to do that, but something had to be done ; so he took Vijaya and his seven hundred men, had the half of each man's head shaved as a sign of disgrace, and sent them away in a large ship to go wherever they could find a home away from his country.

As Vijaya sailed southwards along the coast of India, searching for a place where he could settle, he began to see how foolish it was to live a lawless life. He was afraid to remain long at any town on the Indian coast, because he could not trust his men ; their wicked deeds would lead to quarrels, and the strange people they met would not hesitate to kill them. So he sailed on till they came to Lanka, where they landed on a wild and lonely spot, near what is now the town of Puttalam. They had had a long voyage, and were utterly worn out with sea sickness and the troubles of their journey. It was very pleasant for them now to lie down and rest on firm land again. When they rose from the ground they found that the reddish soil had stained the palms of their hands. For this reason they are said to have called the place *Tambapanni*, copper-coloured.

We may notice here that afterwards the whole island was known by this name, *Tambapanni*. When the old Greeks and Romans got to know about Ceylon, they changed *Tambapanni* into *Taprobane*. But the name *Ceylon* comes from *Sinhala-dwipa*,—the island of the Sinhala or lion people. Vijaya and his followers were the first *Sinhalese*.

Though when the Sinhalese landed they saw no human beings anywhere near, there were plenty of people living in the island. These people were naturally afraid to come out from their hiding places in the jungles till they had found out whether the new-comers would do them harm. One day, a dog was seen by one of Vijaya's company, and he followed it, thinking very wisely that where there were dogs there must also be men and women living. Now Vijaya had given orders that his men were to keep together, for this was a strange country and he did not know what dangers there might be. But the man who followed the dog was too inquisitive to obey orders, and he went on till he came to a tank near which he saw a woman sitting and spinning thread. As she appeared from her dress and occupation to be a religious woman, he thought she was not likely to harm him. He bathed in the tank, and began to pluck some roots for his food. Then suddenly, he found himself caught by the woman, and in spite of all his cries and prayers, he was thrown into a cave under the tank. In the same way she managed to imprison every one of Vijaya's seven hundred men. She was no religious woman, but a native princess, one of the demons (*Rakshasas*) who at that time were believed to inhabit Lanka. Her name was **Kuveni**.

When Vijaya found that his men had gone out and did not return, he was alarmed, and arming himself went to look for them. He too came to the place where his followers had been captured, and there he found foot-prints which all led into the tank; but there were no footprints to show that any man had come out. Kuveni also was sitting there as before, spinning thread under the shade of a banyan tree. He at once guessed that she was a Rakshasa and that she had taken his men. "Woman," said he, "hast thou seen my attendants?" "What need hast thou, Prince, of attendants?" she replied. Vijaya was surprised that the woman knew his rank, and was now quite sure that she was a demon. He caught her by the neck and threatened to kill her with his sword if she did not give him back his men. She promised to do so if he would make her his queen. This he did, and there was great rejoicing when the seven hundred men met their prince again.

V.

HOW VIJAYA BECAME KING OF LANKA.

Vijaya had a reason for agreeing to make Kuveni his queen, for he knew that with her help he would be able to conquer the native tribes, and perhaps bring the whole of Lanka under his rule. The Sinhalese found that in the island there were two principal tribes, to whom they gave the names *Yakkhas* (demons) and *Nagas* (snakes); for these tribes seemed to them to be strange and uncivilized people, who could scarcely be considered human beings. The Yakkhas lived chiefly in the hill country towards the middle of the island, and had a city called Lankapura. This will remind us of what we read before about the Rakshasas and their city. The Nagas lived in the northern and western parts of the island; there was a Naga king at Kelaniya.

Kuveni helped Vijaya willingly and well, though he was fighting against her own people. A great wedding feast was going on at Laggala in the hill country, when the son of one Yakkha chief was being married to the daughter of another chief who lived close by. Here was a chance for Vijaya to overcome them easily. Kuveni guided him to the place where the feast was held, and there the Yakkhas were taken by surprise and killed. Other tribes were afterwards conquered, and the Sinhalese saw that they could become masters of the whole country. It was a good land to live in, and they began to make it their own.

Some of Vijaya's seven hundred followers went far inland, and settled in districts over which they ruled as chiefs. But their principal town was Tammana Nuwara, where their leader Vijaya lived. After some time the Sinhalese chiefs met together and decided that they were now strong enough to have a kingdom and king of their own in this new land. They agreed to ask Vijaya to call himself King of Lanka. But Vijaya said he could not do that while Kuveni was his queen; a king should have a queen who was his equal in rank and birth. The chiefs then sent messengers, with valuable presents, according to the custom of the time, to the king of Madura in South India, and asked him to let his daughter be Vijaya's queen. The king was willing to do this and with his daughter he sent also seven hundred ladies of high rank to marry Vijaya's followers. All these ladies belonged to the people known as Pandyans, and Madura was the chief city of the kingdom of Pandya in South India.

When it was known in Lanka that the Indian princess was coming, Vijaya made haste to send Kuveni away. This was a cruel thing to do, but he did it. He had to make some excuse to her, so he said that the new princess was a timid person who would be afraid to live with a demon. "But where can I go?" asked Kuveni. "On thy account have I fought against my own people, so many of whom have been killed. I dare not go back to them; and now thou too turnest me away." Vijaya said she could live anywhere in his dominions where she would be safe from the revenge of the Yakkhas, and he would give her all she wanted. But she proudly refused to accept anything from him, and with her children went weeping to the city of Lankapura, where her relatives lived. Leaving the children outside the walls, she entered the city alone. Here she was at once surrounded by the Yakkhas, who thought she had come again as a spy, and one of them n his anger killed her with a blow. A friendly warning was at once given to the children, and they fled to a place near Adam's Peak where they settled. The Veddas are said to be their descendants.

Vijaya now married the princess who came from Madura, and there was great ceremony and rejoicing when he was made King of Lanka. We may call him the first King of the Sinhalese, and there does not appear to have been any trouble or disturbance during his long reign of thirty-eight years.

V.

THE BUILDING OF ANURADHAPURA

Pandukabhaya, the third king after Vijaya, passed through many dangers and fought many battles before he won the throne of Lanka. He had ten uncles, of whom nine did their best to kill him, for it had been foretold by certain wise Brahmans that he would kill his uncles and become king. When he was born, therefore, his mother deceived the uncles, saying that a daughter was born, and sent her son to a village herdsman who brought him up as his own child.

It is interesting to read of the escapes that Pandukabhaya had. Iu the village where he lived there was a marsh near which the young prince used to play with the village boys as his companions. In this marsh there was a hollow tree, and the prince found a way into the hollow of the tree through an opening which was hidden under the water; but he told nobody about this. When he was about seven years old, his uncles came to hear about him and sent people to make an end of him. One day these people surrounded the marsh where he and the village boys were playing as usual. The prince, finding himself in danger, dived under the water with his clothes on, and hid himself in the hollow of the tree. The other boys were killed, and the people went back to tell the uncles that Pandukabhaya also had been killed, for they counted the clothes left on the bank of the marsh and were satisfied that nobody had escaped.

After some time, news reached the uncles that the prince was still alive, and they thought it would be best to kill all the herdsmen of the village, so as to make sure that the prince could not escape. On the day fixed for this cruel murder, the herdsmen had gone hunting, and they sent the prince to the village for some fire to roast the game they had killed. The prince went, but feeling tired remained in the village, and sent his guardian's own son with the fire. The moment this boy appeared he and the herdsmen were surrounded and put to death. But the prince was again lucky enough to escape.

When he was grown up his mother sent him to a rich and learned Brahman to be educated. The Brahman, who was also an astrologer, saw that his pupil was destined to become King, and soon taught him all that a prince should know, for the prince was a willing and clever pupil.

The time now came when Pandukabhaya was ready to begin his fight for the throne. The Brahman helped him with money as well as with advice, and the prince soon had soldiers enough. He first defeated one of his uncles, whose daughter he married, and who now took his part. The king himself (who was another uncle and who had always been kind to him) found that Pandukabhaya was too strong to be beaten, and offered to divide the kingdom with him, giving the prince all the country south of the Mahaveli Ganga. But the other eight uncles would not agree to this arrangement, and they continued the fighting. A great battle took place at the hill called Ritigala, in which Pandukabhaya was greatly helped by a tribe of Yakkhas whom he had conquered. The eight uncles were defeated and killed, and the victorious prince marched to Anuradhapura where one of his relatives ruled. After a war that had lasted over seventeen years, he was now king of Lanka.

From this time (about 400 years before the birth of Christ), Anuradhapura was the capital of the Sinhalese kings for more than a thousand years. But when Pandukabhaya settled there it was not much more than a village. The king determined to make it a great city. He cleared the land of the jungle that grew over it, made streets, and built several tanks, of which one was called the *Jaya-wewa*, the Lake of Victory. He added four suburbs to the city, marked out the ground for a cemetery, and provided a place of punishment for those who broke the law. He made arrangements to keep the city clean and free from sickness; and as seven hundred scavengers were employed in this work, the number of people in the city must have been very great. The scavengers lived in a separate village not far from where they worked. The former king, Abhaya, was made governor of the city to see that all the laws were obeyed, and that all the work required was done properly.

Pandukabhaya did not forget the Yakkhas who had helped him to gain his throne. They were still a powerful people, far more in number than all the Sinhalese, and the king took care to treat them with respect One of their leaders was given charge of the southern gate of the city, to prevent enemies coming from that direction. The Yakkhas were worshippers of demons, and the king ordered that whatever offerings were required for their worship should be regularly provided year by year. In the same way he provided for people of all other religions who lived at Anuradhapura. As the king himself and the Sinhalese were followers of the Brahman religion, the Brahman priests were freely given temples, dwelling-places, and all else that they needed.

VI.

THE NEW RELIGION

King Tissa was greatly favoured by the gods whom the Sinhalese worshipped. So greatly was he favoured that he came to be known as **Devanam-piya Tissa**, Tissa the Delight of the Devas. On the day he became king it was seen how much these devas loved him, for it is said that they caused wonders to appear on land and sea. The riches that had been hidden in the earth for ages—gold and silver, sapphires, rubies, and other precious stones—came up of their own accord for the king's use and pleasure. The treasures that had been lost in the sea in ships that were wrecked near the coast of Lanka, came up of their own will and spread themselves on the shore. The eight kinds of pearls which men gather with great trouble and danger from the depths of the ocean, rose freely to the surface and ranged themselves in a long line upon the beach On a mountain near Anuradhapura, the capital, another wonder happened. Three graceful bamboo stems sprang up. The first, which shone like silver, was encircled with creeping plants of golden hue. On the second clustered beautiful flowers, full-blown, and of many different colours The third stem was the stem of animals, and on it appeared the forms of various birds and beasts. When Tissa saw these wonderful gifts he said, "My friend Dharmasoka and he only is worthy of such treasures as these. I will send them to him."

Two questions have now to be answered: Why was Tissa so greatly favoured? Who was this friend Dharmasoka? The answer to the first question is that the devas favoured Tissa because he was the first Buddhist king of Lanka. It was in his reign that the Sinhalese began to change their religion from Brahmanism to Buddhism. On that account the priests who wrote about him said all they could in his praise, and described him as the favourite of the gods, who made wonders happen in Lanka when he became king.

To answer the second question we must go back to India. Dharmasoka, or **Asoka**, as he is generally called, was a famous king in Northern India who had become a Buddhist, and who worked hard to teach Buddhism wherever he could. It happened that all his people were not agreed about the teachings of the Buddha, and therefore Asoka made the priests in India meet together at a great council, and there decide what the right teachings of Buddhism were. But another important thing was done at the meeting. Preachers were appointed to go to foreign countries and convert the peoples there to Buddhism. A high honour was kept for Lanka, for the preacher appointed to convert this island was no other than **Mahinda**, who was known as king Asoka's own son.

Carrying out his intention, Devanam-piya Tissa sent Asoka the treasures he had obtained from land and sea in so remarkable a manner, and in turn received costly gifts from the

Indian king. In addition to his gifts Asoka sent his friend this message : "I have taken refuge in the Buddha, in his religion, and in his priesthood. Do thou also take refuge in his salvation." In other words, Asoka said he had become a Buddhist and advised Tissa to become a Buddhist too.

Some time after this exchange of presents took place, Tissa with a great number of attendants was hunting near the Mihintale hill. Following an elk he came to a lonely spot where, to his surprise, he found the elk gone, and in its place, a strange man standing. There were other men too with him, whom the King did not notice at the time. The stranger called to the king "Come here, Tissa." From the familiar way in which he spoke, the king thought that he was one of the friendly Yakkha chiefs; but he soon learnt the truth. "We are the ministers and disciples of the lord of the true faith," said the stranger ; "out of pity for thee, Maharaja, we have come hither from Jambu-dvipa." The lord of the true faith was, of course, the Buddha, and Jambu-dvipa was an old name for India ; the stranger was Mahinda himself, the son of the great Asoka. Tissa remembered at once the message he had received from the Indian king. He laid aside his bow and arrow, and sitting near Mahinda talked a long while about the new religion. The result was that Tissa and the thousands who accompanied him to Mihintale became Buddhists. Mahinda and the other preachers then came to Anuradhapura, where a suitable dwelling-place was provided for them in the king's garden, away from the noise and business of the city. Every mark of honour and reverence was shewn to them by the king. Whatever they wished was done. Whatever they required was freely given. Buddhism became in a short time the religion of the Sinhalese people, and even many of the Naga tribes accepted the new faith.

VII.

THE GREAT VIHARA

Now that Buddhism had become the religion of the Sinhalese, it was necessary that places should be set apart for worship and for the residences of the priests and their attendants. The priests loved to dwell in quiet places, undisturbed by the hurry and excitement of men engaged in business or pleasure; places well provided with shade and water, where they could walk or sit and think about sacred things, and where they could train their pupils in the teachings of the Buddha. Tissa talked over the matter with Mahinda, and then agreed to mark out a portion of land which should ever after be sacred to the new religion. The day on which this marking out was done was made a great holiday. Notice of it was given to the people by beat of drums. On the appointed morning the king came dressed in his grandest robes, riding in his royal chariot, and escorted by companies of soldiers. He went first to the temple where the priests lived, and with them went to the spot where the marking was to begin. The whole city, every house and every street, was gaily decorated with flags and wreaths of flowers. Great arches of honour were put up at various places through which the grand procession should pass. Crowds of people cheered the king, the priests, the soldiers and the great ladies who went to the marking out of the boundaries. The marking was done with a golden plough, drawn by two of the king's elephants, and the king himself held the plough.

When the ground had been marked out, a Vihara, or monastery for the priests, was built within the boundary, with halls for preaching and for meditation, with bathing places, and with rooms for use by night and by day. This vihara became very famous afterwards, and was known as the **Maha Vihara**. It is spoken of as "a great seat of learning and the home of great men."

The next thing required was a relic of the Buddha. Mahinda pointed out that there were no relics in Lanka to which the people could make offerings, and he advised Tissa to ask for some from India. Messengers were at once sent to Asoka, who gladly sent to Lanka the right collar-bone of the Buddha and a bowlful of other relics. A great dagaba was then built over the spot where the collar-bone relic was placed. This was the **Thuparama Dagaba**, the first dagaba that was built in Lanka.

So many women were converted to Buddhism that special attention had to be paid to them. The Princess Anula, wife of the king's younger brother, was one of the converts, and she with five hundred of her ladies asked permission to enter the priesthood. Mahinda told the king that he had no power to ordain them. "We are not allowed to ordain females. In the city of Pataliputta (Patna) there is a priestess. She is my younger sister, renowned under the name of **Sanghamitta**, and profoundly learned. Write, king, to our royal father, begging that he may send her, and with her the right branch of the bo-tree of the lord of saints,—itself the monarch of the forests. She will ordain these females."

When the request was made to Asoka he was naturally unwilling to part with his daughter ; but as she felt it her duty to leave her parents and her home for the sake of her religion, she was at length allowed to go. She brought with her the branch of the bo-tree under the shade of which the Buddha had found salvation, and which was therefore sacred to all Buddhists. She was received here with the highest honour, and the sacred branch was reverently taken to Anuradhapura and planted in the great garden attached to the Maha Vihara. And there the tree stands to this day, perhaps the oldest tree in the world.

The princess Anula and her ladies were in due time admitted to the priesthood, and Sanghamitta was as active as her brother in spreading Buddhism throughout this land. For her the king built two viharas. She and Mahinda lived for some years in Lanka after the death of Tissa, and when they themselves died, the king of that time had their bodies burned, according to the custom, with all the honour that could be shewn to persons of such high position and of such unselfish and saintly character.

VIII.

THE TAMILS

The Sinhalese kings—not only Devanampiya Tissa, but also those who reigned after him—were so busy attending to the affairs of the new religion that they had very little time for other important duties. They could think of little besides building viharas for their priests. One king built as many as five hundred "delightful" viharas in various parts of the island. While he spent his time in this work, some of the Sinhalese princes went away from Anuradhapura and made themselves chiefs of places far from the capital,—in places like Kelaniya, which was then sixteen miles from the sea, and like Magama in Ruhuna, the name of that part of the island which lay south of the Mahaveli Ganga and the Kalu Ganga. Here they ruled as if they were independent kings, and they became even strong enough to disobey the king of Lanka. But a worse danger came to the Sinhalese people. The Tamils of South

India often visited the island, and they saw what was going on. They noticed that the Sinhalese king delighted in acts of religion, but neglected to train soldiers for war, or to build forts and other defences against enemies. It soon happened that two bold Tamil chiefs came over with ships and horsemen, and, putting the Sinhalese king to death, reigned in Anuradhapura. The Sinhalese of Anuradhapura had forgotten how to fight, and it took them twenty years to get rid of these Tamils. Then after a peace of ten years, another Tamil chief came over, a prince named **Elāra**, with a large Tamil army. He took Anuradhapura, and reigned there for forty-four years. He could not conquer the kings of Kelaniya and Ruhuna, but he made them pay him tribute year by year, and acknowledge him as king of Lanka.

Elāra built forts instead of dagabas and viharas. He was a Brahman by religion, and as he was a stranger in Lanka he wisely thought first of protecting himself from the attacks of the people he had conquered. But he also tried to please the Sinhalese and make them content to live under his rule. He was just in his dealings, and treated the Sinhalese in the same way as he treated his own Tamils. Though he was not a Buddhist, he respected the Buddhist religion, and gave what money and other gifts were wanted to support the Buddhist priests and their viharas.

He also brought into Lanka a strange custom which was practised by some of the princes of Southern India. Over his bed he hung a bell which had a long rope tied to it, the end of the rope being at the palace gate; all those who wished to complain to the king himself had only to ring the bell, and the king himself would then attend to their complaint. Some curious stories are told about this bell. Once a snake climbed up a palmyra tree and swallowed a young bird which was there. The mother-bird flew to the bell-rope and pulled it. King Elāra made enquiries, and had the serpent brought to him; when it was cut open the bird was found inside. The snake was then hung up on the palmyra tree.

At another time, an old woman laid her paddy out to dry, and it was wet by an unexpected shower of rain. Taking the paddy with her she went and rang the bell. The king was puzzled over this thing. Why should the rain have damaged the paddy? "When a king rules righteously," he said, "the rain ought to fall at proper times." He sought the help of the devas by making offerings to them and by fasting; and on account of his well-known piety and love of justice the devas so ordered it that rain should fall only once a week, in the middle of the night, and then in such showers that the ponds and wells should everywhere be filled.

These stories shew us what people thought of Elāra's character. But we must not forget that Elāra was not a Buddhist, though he was kind to the Sinhalese and their religion. Nor can we forget that he depended for his safety on his Tamil soldiers, who were not as friendly to the Sinhalese and their religion as the king himself was. We may suppose therefore that quarrels would frequently arise between the Sinhalese and the Tamils, especially when the Tamils offered any insult or harm to the dagabas or to the Buddhist priests. Besides, most of the Sinhalese could not like the rule of a king who was not of their own race or religion. Some of them did, because they were comfortable and held high positions, and so long as they themselves had all they wanted they did not care who governed the country or how the rest of the people were treated. But there were many others of a better sort, who were angry at the shame that had fallen on their land and people, and who were anxious to drive the Tamils out of the island. Most of these patriots lived in the province of Ruhuna, and about one of them we shall now hear.

IX.

THE UNDUTIFUL PRINCE

While Elara reigned at Anuradhapura the descendants of the Sinhalese kings lived and ruled in other parts of the island. Ruhuna was governed by Kavan Tissa, who kept companies of soldiers as guards at all the ferries by which the Great River was crossed, so that the Tamils might be kept from coming over ; but he was not bold enough or strong enough to march across the river and fight against Elāra. He had two sons whom he named Gemunu and Tissa. Their mother was Vihara Devi, a gentle and beautiful princess, who came to Ruhuna in a rather remarkable way. Her father, the king of Kelaniya, had done a wrong to the priesthood, and as a punishment for this, his province was flooded by the sea, and he was commanded to give up his daughter to the sea. The princess was placed in a boat and set adrift. By good luck the currents brought her to Magama on the south-eastern coast, the capital of Ruhuna, where she was rescued. As the princess came ashore near a vihara, she was given the name of *Vihara Devi*.

Gemunu and Tissa were educated like other princes of the time in all warlike arts, and their pious father took care that they were also well instructed in the teachings of Buddhism. But even as children the brothers were vexed at the thought of the Tamils holding the land over which Sinhalese kings had ruled. Their father suspected this, and feared that they might lose their lives in rashly trying to fight against the Tamils. One day, when Gemunu was twelve, and Tissa ten years old, he put them to a test. He placed boiled rice before them in a golden dish, and divided the rice into three portions. He gave them one portion saying, "Eat this, vowing ye will never do injury to the priests;" then another portion, saying, "Eat this, vowing ye two brothers will always live in friendship." The boys willingly ate both the portions of rice, and so far the king was satisfied. Then he gave them the remaining portion and said. "Eat this, vowing ye will never make war against the Tamils." This the boys angrily refused to do. Tissa threw away the portion given to him; so did Gemunu, who immediately after went to his bed and curled himself on it. His mother, seeing that something had gone wrong, followed, and found him in this unusual position. She said gently, "My boy, why dost thou not stretch thyself on thy bed and lie down comfortably?" "How can I, mother?" replied Gemunu; "the great sea presses on me on one side, and the Tamils across the river press on me on the other side; how can I lie down with limbs outstretched?"

This one thought of driving out the Tamils filled Gemunu's mind, and for that task he prepared himself. He learnt the use of the bow and the lance, the management of the elephant and the horse. He studied the art of war. Then he gathered round him a chosen company of ten mighty warriors, each famous in his own way. For instance, Nandi-mitta, though he lived at Anuradhapura where his father was one of Elara's ministers, would tear in two any Tamil who dared to insult the Buddhist sacred buildings. Sura-nimila was by nature lazy; but he once travelled thirty miles between dawn and sunrise to deliver an important message. Velu-Sumana was a splendid horseman. Leaping on the back of a charger which no other man could mount, he urged him to full speed, and went round and round so fast that it seemed as if there was but one long horse in every part of the circus. And so it was with the other seven; they were able to perform wonderful deeds which we can hardly believe, and each hero, it is said, had the strength of ten elephants!

The prince's army was collected in this way. Each of the ten heroes enlisted ten men; that made a hundred and ten. Each of the hundred another ten; each of the thousand another ten. The total number was 11,110, and all were picked warriors.

Gemunu was now eager to attack the Tamils. He felt sure that his army was strong enough to drive them out of the country. But king Kavan Tissa was not so sure, and he was afraid that his son's life might be lost in a foolish war. Besides, was not Ruhuna sufficient for a king to rule over? So he would not allow a war to be begun. Three times Gemunu begged for permission to fight the Tamils, but all in vain. Then the young prince lost his temper, and accused his father of shameful cowardice. He was rude enough to send his father a woman's ornament to wear, saying: "If my father were a man, he would not refuse my request; so let him wear this." Then to avoid his father's just anger, he fled to the Malaya district, the hill-district near Adam's Peak and was ever afterwards known as **Dutu-Gemunu**, Gemunu the Undutiful.

X.

THE DEFEAT OF ELARA

It was not till after his father's death that Gemunu returned to Ruhuna; but before he could reach Magama his younger brother Tissa had set himself up as king and was supported by a large number of people. He was strong euough to defeat Gemunu in the first battle fought between the brothers; but in the next battle his army was badly beaten and he had to fly for safety to the priests who hid him in their viharas till Gemunu's anger was cooled. The brothers were afterwards friendly.

Dutu-Gemunu was now king of Ruhuna, and he was free to begin the great war for which he had so long and so anxiously prepared himself. He had a very large army; he had also the favonr of the priests, and the good wishes of his people. There was no reason for delay.

Starting from Magama, he pushed on to Mahiyangana (in the present Bintenne District) and captured it from the Tamils. Then he tried to cross the Mahaveli Ganga, but the ferry was so strongly guarded by the Tamils that it was not till after four months of fighting that he succeeded in getting through. Fort after fort beyond the river now fell into Gemunu's hands, and the Tamils fled into the town of Vijitapura, near Polonnaruwa, where they hoped to be able to defend themselves. Vijitapura was a strongly fortified town, only less strong than Anuradhapura itself. Three moats or wide ditches filled with water surrounded it, and there was also a strong wall round the city, with four huge iron gates eighteen cubits high.

It took four months of fighting before Gemunu was able to enter Vijitapura—so fierce was the resistance of the Tamils. Each of the four gates was attacked by the Sinhalese, but the principal fight was at the southern gate where Nandi-mitta and Sura-nimila, with Kandula, the King's favourite elephant, were doing their best to force an entrance. The elephant charged at the iron gate. but the Tamils from the watch-tower above flung down spears, hot lumps of iron, and a stream of melted resin which burned like fire on the back of the noble beast. Kandula was maddened by the pain and rushed into the moat to cool his tortured body. The keepers dressed his wounds, and protected his body with a covering of buffalo hides over which was spread an oiled skin. Then Kandula charged again at the gate. "Roaring like the thunder of heaven, and daring all danger, with his tusks he shivered the gate; with his foot battered the threshold; and the gate fell together with its door and bolts with a tremendous crash. Nandi-mitta opposing his shoulder to the mass of materials falling from the watch-tower over the elephant hurled it inwards." (*Mahavansa*). The victorious Sinhalese entered the city, put to death all the Tamils they met, and broke down the defences which had kept them out so long.

Two more Tamil chiefs were next overcome, and then Gemunu came before the great city of Anuradhapura. He selected a suitable place for his camp and guarded it with thirty-two lines of defence, he himself remaining within the innermost line. Elara knew that the fight must end in the death of one of the two, since both of them claimed the throne of Lanka. He determined to attack Gemunu, and sent his chief general Dighajantu forward. This brave warrior broke through the outer lines, one by one, and came at last to that which Gemunu defended. Here his good luck left him, and in an encounter with Sura-nimila he was killed. The Tamils, seeing their champion fall, would have fled, but Elara encouraged them to go on fighting and the battle was renewed.

Gemunu rushed forward to meet the Tamil king; "None but I myself shall fight Elara," he commanded. Near the southern gate of the city the rival monarchs met face to face, and the splendid duel was watched by both armies. Each king was mounted on his own elephant. Elara hurled his spear at Gemunu, who avoided it, and drove Kandula full at Elara's elephant. As the two animals met, Gemunu flung his spear at the Tamil king, and both Elara and his elephant fell dead together.

A brave man respects bravery in other men, even in his enemies; and Gemunu did not fail in his duty towards the dead Tamil king. Elara's body was burnt with all the customary honours due to a king, at the place where he died, and a tomb was built over the ashes. Gemunu then ordered that whosoever should at any time pass that tomb, even if he were the king himself, should go on foot and in silence. How well that order was obeyed we may understand from what happened two thousand years after Elara's death. In the year 1818, a Kandyan chief rebelled against the British government and tried to escape by way of Anuradhapura. He was so tired that he could hardly move from the chair on which he was carried. Yet, when he came near Elara's tomb, he got down, and as he did not know the exact spot where the tomb was, he walked on till he had passed far beyond.

After Elara's death, Gemunu ruled as sole sovereign over Lanka. It is true that Elara's nephew came from India with an army to get back the throne; but he was easily defeated, and for sixty years the land had peace.

XI.

THE REIGN OF DUTU-GEMUNU

Two of the finest buildings in old Anuradhapura were planned and set up by Dutu-Gemunu during his twenty-four years of peaceful rule as king of all Lànka. He is said, indeed, to have built ninety-nine viharas which cost him very large sums of money. The Mirisveti Vihara at Anuradhapura was one of these. But the two buildings which have become most famous are the *Brazen Palace* and the *Ruanveli Dagaba.*

The Brazen Palace, or, as it is properly called, the *Lowa Maha Paya*, was built near the Maha Vihara as a dwelling place for its priests. It stood on 1,600 pillars of granite—forty rows of forty pillars in each row. Most of these pillars, rising twelve feet above the ground, may still be seen, and they are all that remain of this remarkable building. The palace was 100 cubits lcng, 100 cubits broad, and 100 cubits high. It had nine storeys one over the other, with 100 richly-decorated rooms in each storey. The priests of highest merit lived in the four highest storeys, and the lower ones were occupied by the priests according to their different grades, so that the priests of lowest rank had rooms on the lowest floor The roof of the palace was covered with sheets of brass, and that is why it came to be called the Brazen Palace.

In the middle of this palace was a hall standing on gilt pillars built in the shape of lions and other animals; and in the centre of this hall there was a throne of ivory on which was placed an ivory fan of rich beauty. The fan was a sign of the priesthood. Above the throne shone a white umbrella which was the Sinhalese sign of royalty. We are to understand from this that as the umbrella covered the fan, so the king of Lanka protected the priests and the Buddhist religion.

The Ruanveli Dagaba is known as the *Maha Thupa* (the Great Dagaba), and was the grandest building till then seen in Lanka. This was the building to which Gemunu gave the best of his thought and time, and on which he prided himself most. Very carefully were the foundations prepared, and the "festival-brick" was laid with great ceremony. All round the site the place was gaily decorated; so were the roads leading to it; and so was the capital itself. The king went there in stately procession, attended by his ministers dressed in their rich robes of office, and by chosen companies of soldiers. Dancing and singing women, with a full band of musicians accompanied him. The streets were crowded with a delighted people, and with priests in thousands, some of them coming from India, all assembled to do honour to their religion.

Another festival like this, perhaps a grander one, took place later when the relics were solemnly placed in the shrine made for them in the middle of the Dagaba. In the shrine there was also a bo-tree made of gold and silver and precious stones, and round it were golden images of the Buddha and of others whom the Buddhists worshipped. The Dagaba was 120 cubits high. No forced labour was employed in building it, nor was forced labour employed for the Brazen Palace. The war with the Tamils had cost the people so much money that the king could not ask them for more. All workmen were therefore paid for their work.

And now we came to one of the most touching stories recorded in the old books—the death of Dutu-Gemunu. The great Dagaba was nearly finished; only the spire and the plastering of the walls remained to be done. Then the king fell ill. He was so anxious to see how the building would look when it was completed, that a false spire of bamboo-work was put up and the walls were covered with white cloth. The sick king was then carried to a spot from where he was able to see on his right hand the Maha Thupa, and on his left the Lowa Maha Paya. There, for a while he bowed in worship amidst a crowd of priests. The priest Theraputtabhaya, who had formerly been one of his ten chosen warriors, stood near his dying leader. "In times past," said the king, "I was supported by thee in war; now single-handed must I begin my fight with Death. This enemy I shall not be able to overcome."

"Maharajah," replied the priest, "the power of Death cannot be overcome unless the enemy Sin is first subdued. Call to mind thy many acts of piety, and comfort shall surely be given thee."

The secretary was commanded to bring the register of the king's pious deeds, and to read aloud the long list of viharas and other buildings made by the king; of the numerous festivals duly observed; of the arrangements made for regular religious preaching; of the garments, food, and gifts bestowed on the priests; and of the hospitals built and endowed for the poor. Gemunu had been indeed, as he himself said, the "slave of the priesthood,"—so much had he done for them.

But the comfort he obtained from the recital of his good deeds was small. "All these things." he said, were given when I was prosperous. The thought of them gives me no relief. Only two offerings made when I was in adversity bring comfort to my mind."

He called his brother Tissa to him, and gave him directions as to how the Maha Thupa was to be completed, and bade him keep up the regular offerings to the priests. Then he turned to the Dagaba, and, while yet gazing at the noble buildings to which he had devoted the last years of his brave and pious life, the royal patriot died.

XII.

THE ABHAYAGIRI VIHARA

The Tamils of South India could not long keep away from so rich a country as Lanka, and about sixty years after Elara's death they came again to try to win it for themselves.

At that time the king of Lanka was **Valagam Bahu**, and he had been king for only five months when seven Tamil chiefs with their armies landed at Mantota. Valagam Bahu went out to meet them, and a great fight took place at Kolambalaka, a village between Mantota and Anuradhapura, where once before Dutu-Gemunu had defeated a Tamil army. But this time, the Sinhalese were utterly beaten, and the king was forced to flee for safety. One of the Tamil chiefs captured Valagam Bahu's beautiful queen, and with her returned to India. Another of the chiefs went back to India taking with him the eating-bowl of the Buddha, a relic which the Sinhalese valued very highly. The five other chiefs stayed in Lanka and, one after the other, governed the country for nearly fifteen years in all, while the rightful king hid himself in far away jungles and caves where the Tamils could not reach him.

When Valagam Bahu fled from the Tamils he left Anuradhapura through a gate near which some Hindu priests lived. As he fled, one of these priests, named Giri, rudely laughed at him, crying out, "The great black Sinhala is flying!" Now, it is bad enough to mock people who are in trouble, but this man was ungrateful as well as rude; for it was by the king's favour that he and others who were not Buddhists were allowed to follow their own religion in Lanka. The king noticed the insult, but could do nothing at the time to punish the man.

Some, at all events, of the Buddhist priests were loyal to their king. One, whom he met in the jungles near Adam's Peak, gave him food to eat when he was hungry. Valagam Bahu had no way of rewarding the priest except this: he wrote on the leaf of a tree that certain lands should be set apart for the priest when the Tamils were overcome. Thus began the custom of giving lands for the support of the priesthood.

The five Tamil chiefs did not keep their power very long. Each reigned at Anuradhapura for a short period and was then killed by the king who reigned after him. When the last of the Tamils was reigning, Valagam Bahu was ready to fight again. Two Buddhist priests were specially active in working for him. They stirred up the people in his favour, pointing out that Valagam Bahu would be a better friend of Buddhism than the Tamils. A Sinhalese army was collected, and, putting himself at his head, Valagam Bahu marched to Anuradhapura, defeated and killed the Tamil chief, and again ruled over his own people.

The king was now able to reward those who had been faithful to him and to punish his enemies. Several viharas were built for the faithful priests. One of them was the splendid **Abhaya giri Vihara**, which was built on the ground where formerly stood the temple of Giri, the Hindu priest who insulted the king. The name of the vihara was formed from *Abhaya* (part of the king's name and *Giri*.

This new vihara was larger than the old Maha Vihara, and a dispute unfortunately arose between the priests of the two places. One of the Maha Vihara priests was expelled for breaking the rule of the monastery, and a pupil of the expelled priest was so annoyed at this that he went over to the Abhaya-giri Vihara and joined that brotherhood. Thus began a separation between the Viharas which lasted for eleven hundred years.

Another vihara that we may note is the one at Dambulla, where the king once hid himself during his fifteen years' flight from the Tamils. All that can be now seen of it is a number of gloomy caves built half-way up the side of an enormous mass of rock. The largest of these rock caves is full of statues and paintings. There is a large statue of Valagam Bahu and another of the Buddha. Indeed, there are over fifty statues of the Buddha in the cave, and the roof and walls are covered with paintings which celebrate events in the history of Lanka —such as the landing of Vijaya, the great duel between Elara and Dutu-gemunu, and the bringing into Lanka of the sacred Bo-tree.

There is one other important event which we must notice in connection with the reign of Valagam Bahu. The Maha Vihara priests were afraid, after what had happened at the Abhaya-giri Vihara, that the true doctrines of Buddhism would be wrongly understood and taught if they were not written down in books. All this time they had been taught orally They met therefore, at Aluvihara, near Matale, and wrote down in the Pali language three collections of Buddha's teachings—the *Tripitaka* —with notes and explanations of them in Sinhalese. We shall see later on how fortunate it was that this was done.

Valagam Bahu reigned twelve years after he got back his throne.

XIII.

THE BLIND MUSICIAN

In a certain part of South India there is said to have lived a very clever musician who was, however, blind and almost entirely dependent on what his wife was able to earn. No doubt the poor woman had a hard time of it, and she would often say unkind things to her husband because he did not help her in getting money for the daily wants of the house. Still, she ought to have remembered that he was blind. He grew weary at length of their continual quarrels, and one day he told her that he would not trouble her any longer as he was going away to Lanka!' "Oh!" she said, mocking him; "so you are going to Lanka! I suppose you expect to get a tusked elephant and rich estates there!"

This blind musician may have come to Lanka—if he came at all—at the time when one of the five Tamils was reigning at Anuradhapura, and the Sinhalese king Valagam Bahu was hiding in the jungles of the hill country. The musician asked to be taken into the presence of the Tamil king, but this could not be allowed, as it was thought unlucky for a king to see a blind man. But the story he gave of himself was a strange one, and many people were there who spoke of his wonderful skill in music. The king was curious to meet him and the ministers arranged that the king should hear him sing and play on his lyre without seeing him at all. The musician was taken to a room across which a thick curtain was drawn, and behind the curtain was the king; this the musician did not know, or, at all events, was not told.

His skill in music and his cleverness as a poet were now to be tested. Hidden by the curtain, the king took off the royal robes he wore, and stood in the dress of an archer with a bow and arrow in his hand. The blind poet knew in some way of the change that had been made, and at once sang a verse of his own making in which he compared the king to the great Rama who defeated Ravana. Rama, as we know, was famous for his skill in the use of the bow. Then the king changed his dress and put on the robes of his queen. The musician was ready with another verse which shewed that he knew how the king was now dressed. Last of all, the king wore his own robes, and again the musician sang to the music of his lyre a verse in praise of the ruler of the country.

There was now no doubt in the king's mind that the strange musician was a man of no ordinary ability. Everybody praised him and gave him rich presents. And what, do you think, was the present that the king gave him? Nothing less than a tusked elephant and the ownership of the whole of the northern part of Lanka! The musician's wife in India must have been greatly astonished when she came to hear of her husband's wonderful good fortune.

At that time the peninsula in the north of Lanka was a sandy jungle known as *Manattidal*, the sand-heap. Very few people lived there. The musician sent to South India for people of his own race to come over and settle in his new land where there was plenty of room for them. Many came and lived under the musician who became their king. The people prospered and their numbers increased. The place itself began to be famous, and men spoke of it as *Yalpanam-nadu,* the land of the lyre-poet,—from *Yal* a lyre, or harp, and *Panam* a poet. The Tamils still call it by this name, which the Europeans who afterwards came to Lanka, changed into *Jaffna.*

Such is said to have been the beginning of the Tamil kingdom of Jaffna, for a kingdom it soon became, though we need not believe that the story of the blind musician is actually a true story. The Sinhalese tried to get Jaffna back for themselves, but the Tamils there were too strong. As time went on, fresh bands of Tamils came constantly, and there were other Tamils who had already settled in other parts of Lanka. Between Jaffna and Anuradhapura the land was held by Tamils called *Vanniyar*, and what is called the *Vanni* is the land where the Vanniyar lived. These people had chiefs of their own, and as they grew richer and more numerous they became prouder, and gave much trouble to Sinhalese kings.

What we have specially to note is that so early in the history of Lanka the Tamils had formed a settlement and kingdom of their own in the north of the Island. They were different from the Sinhalese in race, in religion, and in customs, and with the Sinhalese they were continually at war.

XIV.

THE RESULT OF A JOKE

We must not suppose that the old kings of Lanka were always dull and serious and that they had no laughter or amusement. One of these kings found much enjoyment in a joke which, however, ended badly for him.

A gate-keeper of the king's palace, named **Subha**, was employed as one of the king's messengers, to wait at the gate and to go on the king's errands. Subha happened to be very like the king in features and in his appearance generally, and the fun-loving king saw that here was an excellent chance to amuse himself at the expense of his solemn and stately courtiers. He would change places with his messenger. He made Subha put on the royal robes and sit on the throne, while the king himself put on the messenger's turban and stood at the gate with the gate-keeper's staff in his hand. When the chiefs came as usual to pay their respects to the king, they bowed down to Subha, believing that it was the king to whom they bowed. We may well imagine how the king laughed to himself when he saw his proud chiefs bowing before a gate-keeper. The joke was so good that he repeated it several times.

But even kings must be careful not to carry a joke too far. Subha was a clever man, and as bold as he was clever. He quickly saw that he could use the king's folly to benefit himself. Perhaps also, the chiefs did not like being deceived and humbled in this way Anyhow it happened one day, while Subha was on the throne and the king was quietly laughing at the chiefs bowing before him, that the pretended king angrily exclaimed, "How dare that slave laugh in my presence?" The real king was astonished, and tried in vain to prove that the man on the throne was only a servant. All his explanations were useless and he was taken away and put to death for daring to laugh in the royal presence. Subha was accepted by the chiefs as their king, and he reigned six years He was afterwards killed by a young chief who belonged to the family of the old kings.

The son of the new king reigned afterwards as **Vanka-nasika Tissa** (Tissa of the Crooked

Nose), and his queen was the daughter of Subha. He reigned for three years only, and during his reign the Tamils again troubled the country. They came in such numbers that they were able to plunder the land and take away twelve thousand prisoners to India. There was much suffering in Lanka on account of this Tamil invasion, and great was the sorrow of those whose relatives were carried away.

The next king was **Gaja-Bahu**, the first of that name. He was walking through the streets of Anuradhapura one night when he heard a woman weeping in her house. The noise of her grief touched the king's heart and he wondered why she wept. He said to himself, "Some wrong has been done in this city" and he determined to enquire into the matter. He marked with a piece of chalk the door of the house and went back to his palace.

Next day he called his ministers and asked them about the condition of the people in the city. Were there any good or evil deeds of special importance that had been done lately? "O great king," replied the ministers, who wished to flatter him, and shew that the people had nothing to complain of under his rule, "O great king, the city is as happy as a wedding house." Gaja-Bahu who knew better was naturally very angry when he heard this untruth. He sent for the woman whom he had heard crying the previous night and asked her why she was so unhappy. She said that her two sons were among the prisoners taken to India by the Tamils.

Gaja-Bahu saw that it would not do to let the Tamils go unpunished and he made preparations for war. When he was quite ready, he went over to South India with his famous general, *Nila*, and a large army, and so thoroughly frightened the Tamil king there, that not only were the twelve thousand Sinhalese prisoners released, but an equal number of Tamil prisoners were brought over to Lanka. These Tamils were placed in various parts of the Kandy, Colombo, and Kurunegala districts—in the Alutkuru Korale, Tumpane, Harispattu, etc.

The king brought back also the eating-bowl of the Buddha, which had been taken away in Valagam-Bahu's time, and a great quantity of jewels and other plunder. In honour of his success he ordered a Perahera to be celebrated every year at Anuradhapura, and this was the beginning of the annual procession which is now seen best in Kandy. But Gaja-Bahu does not seem to have been much liked by the priests of his time, for he was not a strict Buddhist. When he was in India he gave offerings to the Hindu gods, and when he returned to Lanka he encouraged some of the ceremonies and offerings which belonged to the Hindu religion.

XV.

ATTANAGALLA

A few miles from the Veyangoda railway station you will see a high rock on which stands a vihara. It is known as the Attanagalla Vihara. There died a king—and this is his story.

Three friends, who belonged to a powerful tribe in Lanka called the Lambakarnas, were walking by the side of the Tisa Wewa near Anuradhapura. They had come from Mahiyangama (in Bintenna) to perform their duties to the king.

A blind man, who was able to tell beforehand what would happen in the future, heard the sound of the footsteps of the three friends as they walked along the road. He cried out, "Here come three lords who will afterwards reigns as kings of Lanka." One of the chiefs whose name was Gothabhaya, and who happened to be walking behind the other two, overheard this prophecy. He came back alone to the blind man and asked him, "Which of the three shall reign longest ?" The blind man replied, "He who walked behind the others." Gothabhaya returned to his friends, but said nothing of this to them.

The three chiefs were well received by the king and were appointed to high positions in the government. But they soon turned against him, and put him to death.

Then one of the three named **Sangha-Tissa** became king and reigned for four years. He had a curious liking for the jambu fruit, and used to visit an island where grew the jambus he liked best. These visits were very annoying to the villagers, for the king and his ministers forced them to give up a good deal of money and other things at each visit. They therefore cunningly poisoned the jambus intended for the king, who ate them and died.

The next king was **Siri Sangabo**, a very religious man but much too tender-hearted to be a strong ruler. Early in his reign there was a long drought which brought sickness and suffering on the land. It is said that on account of the king's remarkable piety and in answer to his prayers, heavy showers of rain fell and lessened the misery of the people. Then came another trouble, the plague of the Red Eyes. It was probably brought in by the Yakkha tribes, and it was a terrible sickness which began with a redness of the eyes and ended suddenly in death. Men would meet as usual, notice the redness in one another's eyes, and at once drop down dead. The king was bitterly grieved at the loss of so many lives. He was willing to give up his own life if by that means the plague could be stayed; but there was no need for that, as the plague ceased when the king ordered offerings of rice to be made to the demons worshipped by the Yakkhas. This was the beginning of "devil-dancing" ceremonies and *Bali* offerings among the Sinhalese people.

Siri Sangabo could not bear to cause the death of any living thing. He would even strain the water he drank so that he should not swallow the tiny animals which lived unseen in it. He would not put criminals to death but when these were sentenced to be burnt, he would secretly let them escape, and order the bodies of other people who had died natural deaths to be thrown instead into the fire.

A king so indulgent could not expect to reign very long, for those who rule men need to be strong as well as pious, and wise as well as just It is not surprising that he reigned two years only, in spite of his kindness and his piety.

The last of the three Lambakarna chiefs who came from Bintenna to Anuradhapura was Gothabhaya. In Siri Sangabo's reign he held the office of King's Treasurer. He now thought that the time had come when he might safely attempt to gain the throne for himself. He left Anuradhapura, got together a large army, and marched against the king. Siri Sangabo, who hated the shedding of blood, would allow no one to fight for him, and refusing all company left the capital secretly, and came alone southward. All he took with him was his water-strainer, so that when he drank water he might avoid killing the little animals in it.

The new king, **Gothabhaya** reigned at Anuradhapura while the pious Siri Sangabo hid himself at Attanagalla, far away. Here he met a poor villager whose meal of rice he shared. As they talked together it came out that the new king had promised a great reward to anyone who would bring him the head of Siri Sangabo. The reward was so large that many people had been killed by mistake and their heads taken to the king. Indeed, this poor villager was actually searching for the hidden king in order that he might kill him and win the promised reward, which would help the villager and his family to live in comfort. Siri Sangabo pitied the man, and said to him, "I am Siri Sangabo; take my head, and claim your reward." The villager was so astonished and frightened that he ran away; but Siri Sanga-Bo called him back, and dying where he sat, enabled the villager to take the head to King Gothabhaya, and thus obtain the promised reward.

On the spot where this strange event is said to have happened Gothabhaya built a round relic-house two storeys high, and the place has ever since been held in great reverence.

XVI.

A BUILDER OF TANKS

In places where rain falls irregularly, and where months sometimes pass without any rain at all, it is very necessary to collect in lakes and tanks whatever water can be got from rain and from rivers. People can then depend upon getting sufficient water for drinking and other purposes, especially for watering the rice fields from which they obtain their daily food. It is on this account that the old kings of Lanka were so careful to built tanks as well as dagabas and viharas. Tanks were built from the beginning of Sinhalese times, and some of them were of very great size. In Anuradhapura alone there were the *Abhaya-Wewa*, the *Jaya-Wewa*, the *Gamini-Wewa*, and the *Tisa-Wewa*. But now we come to a king who built no fewer than sixteen tanks in various parts of the Island. His name was **Maha Sena**, or **Maha-Sen**.

The largest of these tanks are the *Kantalai* and the *Minneriya* tanks, both between Dambulla and Trincomalie. Each of them is over twenty miles in circumference but Minneriya is half as large again as Kantalai. Minneriya was perhaps the one that Maha-Sena liked best. He is said to have lived on one of the hills close by while the tank was being built, and he hoped that twenty thousand fields would be supplied by the water it held. A small vihara near the tank was afterwards built in his honour and he is even regarded now as the god of that district. In his temple there was till lately an old iron sword which was spoken of as "the Sword of Maha Sena;" it has since disappeared

The Minneriya tank was formed by blocking up the Kara Ganga, so that its waters might run into the tank. Demons were said to have been employed at night to build this and the other tanks, while human beings worked by day; but the demons were only the Yakkhas, whom the Sinhalese found in Lanka when Vijaya came. The king employed them in his service, and for their convenience built a temple where they might worship in their own way.

The reign of Maha-Sena is remarkable in other ways. The king was the younger son of king Goṭhabhaya. When he was a boy he had as his tutor an Indian priest, named *Sangha-Mitta*, who belonged to the Abhaya-Giri Vihara. Now, many of the Abhaya-Giri priests had been driven away to India for teaching things that were contrary to the Buddhism taught in the Maha Vihara. Sangha-Mitta was a pupil and friend of the banished priests, and he taught Maha-Sena to like them too. So when Maha-Sena became king, Sangha-Mitta became his chief adviser, and they joined together in putting down the Maha Vihara. First, they ordered that no one should give alms to any Maha Vihara priest. As the priests could not live without the food the people gave them, they were forced to leave the capital and to wander in Ruhuna, in the jungle near Adam's Peak, where the people were less afraid of the king.

For nine years there were no priests in the Maha Vihara and the place was desolate. Then Sangha-Mitta got the king's permission to destroy the old monastery and to use the materials for new buildings in the Abhaya-Giri Vihara. So bold did he become that he pulled down the Great Brazen Palace also, and more than three hundred other sacred buildings, to make the Abhaya-Giri Vihara the most splendid monastery in Lanka. He was on his way to destroy the Thuparama—the oldest dagaba in the island—when he was killed by some men who were angry at the mischief done to the old Maha Vihara.

The king himself was greatly disliked on account of these things, and his chief minister went away to Ruhuna and there raised a large army to begin a rebellion. There would have been war, but the king and the chief minister met and talked over the matter. In the end, the king repented of the evil he had done, and promised to act more wisely in future. He kept his word to some extent. The Maha Vihara buildings were rebuilt, and its priests brought back. But on a portion of its grounds he built the famous *Jetarana* Dagaba and another vihara for a priest for whom he had taken a strange liking. Then he wanted the Maha Vihara priests to give up the land on which the new dagaba and vihara were built. This they refused to do, and for nine months there was a fresh quarrel, which ended when the king again gave way to the Maha Vihara priests.

In spite of his disputes with the Maha Vihara and his dislike of it, King Maha-Sena was undoubtedly a great ruler, who did much to improve the condition of his people. He was religious in his own way, and his public works,—the dagabas, viharas, and tanks he built—are proofs of his greatness. The

Sinhalese historians say that when he died the line of Great Kings—the *Maha Vansa*—ended. Many kings who reigned after him were greater than he in character and in deeds, but they are said to belong to a line of lower rank and of mixed blood, on which account they are called the *Sulu Vansa.*

XVII.

THE TOOTH-RELIC

The *Dalada Maligawa*, or Temple of the Tooth, in Kandy is visited by people from all parts of the world, and Buddhists hold it in the greatest reverence; for here is kept what most Buddhists believe to be a tooth of the Buddha. It is to them a very sacred relic, which was brought to Lanka about sixteen hundred years ago; and this is the story of the tooth as we find it written down.

When the Buddha died and his body was burned according to the usual custom, this tooth was taken to Kalinga, a kingdom on the east coast of India, between the river Kistna and the river Mahanadi. The people of this country were Buddhists at that time, and they gladly received the relic and worshipped it. Here it remained for some eight hundred years.

Then news came to the king of Kalinga that the king of another country was coming with his armies to fight against him and to carry away the tooth. It was doubtful which of the two kings would win in battle. but the King of Kalinga would not risk losing the sacred relic. He called his daughter and her husband to him, and gave them the tooth, telling them that if he was defeated in the war, he would shew a red flag. They were then to disguise themselves as religious beggars and take the relic to his friend **Siri Mevan**, the King of Lanka. It so happened that the king was defeated and Kalinga was taken by the enemy. The red flag was shewn. The princess hid the relic in the folds of her hair, disguised herself and her husband, and journeyed slowly by land to Tuticorin, where they took ship and came to Lanka.

King Siri Mevan was delighted when he received the sacred gift brought to him. He rewarded the prince and princess with many rich presents and provided for them a palace in which they might live according to their rank. The relic itself was reverently placed in a stone casket of great purity, and carefully guarded in one of the old buildings, which became known as the "House of the Tooth." A number of villages were set apart and the money received from them by the king was used to pay for the proper care of the relic. Once every year a great festival was held in honour of it, when it was taken in procession from its shrine to the Abhay-Giri Vihara.

What happened afterwards to the relic may as well be told here. For very many years it was regarded as one of the two most sacred relics in Lanka—the Buddha's eating-bowl being the other. Anything that touched it was considered to be made holy by the touch. The king who possessed it was considered the rightful Lord of Lanka. Its removal from one place to another was the occasion of grand ceremonies. More than once enemies of the king of Lanka carried it away as part of the plunder they obtained in war; and then there was mourning in Lanka till it was got back. Some six hundred years ago, when Yapahu, in the present North-Western Province, was the capital of the Sinhalese kings, the Tamils made war against the king and carried away the tooth-relic with other treasures. The king was not strong enough to get it back by fighting. He therefore visited the Tamil king in India, some time afterwards, and made himself so agreeable during the visit that the Tamil gave back the relic without any trouble.

When the Portuguese—a people of Europe, about whom we shall learn a great deal shortly—were in Lanka, the Kandyans tried hard to drive them out. A Kandyan chief went to Jaffna to get help from the Tamils there, and took with him the tooth-relic and other valuables for safe keeping. But he was killed in a quarrel that happened to take place in Jaffna, and the tooth fell into the hands of the Jaffnese. Many years later, when the Portuguese took Jaffna, the tooth came into their hands.

The Portuguese took the relic to Goa, their head-quarters in India, and when the Buddhists heard of it, they did all they could to get it back. The king of Pegu (in Lower Burma) offered money to the value of about £50,000, besides promising to supply provisions whenever required for the Portuguese fort of Malacca. The Portuguese Viceroy wished to accept this offer, especially as his Government were at that time in great need of money. But the Roman Catholic Archbishop of Goa would not hear of it. He said he could not encourage the worship of idols, and that it was a sin for Christians to take money and allow a wrong thing to be done. It was then determined to destroy the relic, and this was done publicly and with much ceremony. On the appointed day a crowd assembled and the work of destruction began. The Viceroy threw the relic into a brazen mortar, and the Archbishop himself ground it to powder and then strewed the dust on a heap of burning coals. The whole mass of coals and ashes was then thrown into a river.

But was it the real tooth-relic that was destroyed on that occasion? There are some Buddhists who say that it was only the tooth of a monkey, worshipped by the Hindus of Jaffna, that the Portuguese destroyed. Others believe that when the coals and ashes were flung into the river, a lotus flower in the water opened out its petals and reverently received the sacred ashes which were then by a miracle turned again into the relic. The lotus floated down to the sea, and brought the sacred treasure again to Lanka.

At all events, there is now a tooth-relic—false or true—in the Dalada Maligawa at Kandy

XVIII.

THE ROYAL PHYSICIAN

For about two hundred years after the death of Gaja-Bahu 1. the Sinhalese people were to some extent free from the attacks of the Tamils. During this time of peace much attention was given to the building of tanks and viharas and to the preaching of Buddhism. But the people began also to improve their minds by the study of books—not printed books, of course, for the art of printing was not then known in Lanka—and by the study of such arts as painting, and carving in wood, stone, and ivory. The temples were now richly decorated, and the king's palaces were made beautiful with carved work of all kinds. Images of the Buddha were cut in stone and moulded in silver and gold. A golden image of Mahinda, who brought Buddhism into Lanka, was carried in procession through the streets of Anuradhapura.

We come now to a king who was very famous both as a physician and as a surgeon. His name was **Buddha-Dasa**, which means "the Slave of the Buddha." He seems to have had a great fondness for the study of medicine, and became so skilful in his art that he was able to perform cures that his people thought were wonderful. Not human beings only, but snakes and other animals were also relieved of pain by his skill.

Here is one story from the old books, but we need not believe every word of it. One day, Buddha-Dasa was riding on his elephant to the Tisa-Wewa, when he saw a large cobra stretched out on an ant-hill. The snake appeared to be suffering great pain and there was a large swelling on its body. As we know, the Buddhists regard the cobra as a sacred animal, but on the other hand, they are afraid to go near it. The king got down from his elephant and said to the cobra, "I know what is wrong with you ; but though you are a noble animal, you are also easily made angry. To touch you is dangerous ; yet without touching you I can do nothing to help you." The cobra understood what was said, and immediately put its head into a hole in the ant-hill. Then the king took his knife from the case of instruments he generally carried with him, cut the sore, and dressed the wound. The cobra was very grateful, and rewarded the king with a valuable gem, which the king gave the Abhayagiri Vihara to be set in the eye of a stone statue of the Buddha there.

There is another story which is more interesting. When the king was once passing in procession through the city, a leper who saw him kept beating the ground noisily with his stick, and abusing the king in violent language. But the king would not allow him to be punished; the man was probably ill rather than wicked. He sent a messenger to find out why the leper behaved in this strange way, and was told that the leper was a madman who thought himself superior to the king, and who hated the king so much that he wished to kill him. The king then gave certain directions to the messenger, who in obedience to them returned to the leper. The messenger pretended that he too had a grudge against the king, and that they could work more successfully against him if they lived together in the same house. The leper believed this story, and went to live in the messenger's house where he was treated most kindly and provided with every comfort. This kindness and comfort in time made the leper less ill-tempered. Little by little the leper found out that he owed to the king all the kindness which was shown to him by the king's messenger. He was angry at first, when this was told him, but he soon became more reasonable. In a short time he soon became one of the king's most loyal and loving subjects; so that when he heard a rumour (which was afterwards proved to be false) of the king's death, he actually died of grief. This story shows us the king's skill in curing diseases of the mind, for the leper's hatred was merely a kind of madness.

Many hospitals were established by Buddha-Dasa. One writer tells us that in every village he stationed a physician, an astrologer, and a learned Buddhist preacher; another tells us that one physician was appointed to every ten villages. In either case, the country was well supplied with medical men. Even elephants and horses had medical men appointed to attend to them, and doubtless other animals had their share of attention as well. Along the principal road in the country, he built and furnished hospitals and resting-places for the lame and the blind. Besides all this, the king wrote a book—the *Sarartha-Sangraha*—in which was set down all that was then known about diseases and the cures for them.

A king so kind to his people could not be careless about his religion. The *Suthras*, or sermons of Buddha, were translated from the Pali language into Sinhalese during his reign. The priests enjoyed as much favour from him as from former pious kings. One special gift to them was the building of a new monastery (the *Monara Pirivena*, or Peacock House) at the Maha Vihara; and for the support of the priests who lived there the profits from two villages were set apart. We cannot be surprised that King Buddha-Dasa is described in the old books as "a mine of virtue and an ocean of riches."

XIX.

TWO STRANGERS WHO CAME TO LANKA

After the death of the Buddha, the missionaries of Buddhism carried their religion into many distant lands, and travelled even so far to the East as China. In one of the provinces of that vast country there lived a Chinaman who gave himself up entirely to a religious life. According to the custom of the Chinese when they became Buddhists, he took a new name to shew that he no longer belonged to his family or to the world, but was beginning his life anew.

Fa Hian was the new name of the Chinaman about whom we shall now read. He became a famous traveller and wrote an account of his travels. He was distressed to find that in his country portions of the sacred books of Buddhism were missing, and he set out to search for complete copies of them in India. In this pilgrimage he was accompanied by a few friends, but it is his own experiences in which we are interested.

Instead of going into India by Tibet—which appears to us the shortest way—he crossed the mountains and deserts north of Tibet and entered Turkistan. Then coming round by Afghanistan, he visited Peshawar and travelled across Northern India, studying carefully the customs and religion of each country he passed through, till he arrived at a town near the mouth of the Ganges. Here he stayed two years copying the sacred books and learning the language in which these books were written. Then he sailed in the company of some merchants and reached a country which he called the "Kingdom of Lions," after a voyage of fourteen days with a favourable wind. This Kingdom of Lions was Lanka, and why it was so called we know already.

Fa Hian stayed two years at Anuradhapura where he made copies of the sacred books of Buddhism. Java was the next place he visited, and between that Island and Canton in China he was nearly thrown into the sea by the sailors during a storm; for they thought that it was his presence in the ship which caused the storm! He reached his home after an absence of fifteen years.

What Fa Hian says about Anuradhapura and its people is worth noting. In his time the Abhaya-giri priests were most in favour with the king. In that vihara there were five thousand priests, while the Maha Vihara had only three thousand. Altogether, there were fifty or sixty thousand priests in Lanka, —so he was told. The king was a devout Buddhist and the ceremonies of Buddhism were carefully observed. Religious services were regularly held, and preachers preached the Law on three fixed days each month to multitudes of the people. The sacred bo-tree, then six hundred years old, was held in great reverence, and pillars were built round it to keep it from falling. The tooth-relic was carefully guarded in a house built specially for it, and once a year it was taken through the streets of Anuradhapura to be worshipped.

The Sinhalese people are described as sincere and reverent followers of the Buddha. For a long time, and because, it is said, the kings were pious, the country had been free from famine or scarcity, and there had been no disorder and no rising against the Government. The capital had many large and beautiful houses, in which lived the chief men and a number of foreign merchants. The streets and lanes were kept in good order, and at the head of each of the four principal streets, halls for preaching had been built.

The priests were exceedingly rich, having most valuable jewels in their treasure-houses. In the Abhaya-giri vihara there was a "Hall of the Buddha" with carved work of gold and silver and other rich ornaments, and an image of the Buddha twenty cubits high, cut out of green jade.

It was when Fa Hian stood looking at this image that something happened which we shall let him describe in his own way:—

"Many years had now passed since Fa Hian left the land of Han (*China.*) The people with whom he had mingled were men of foreign lands. The hills, the rivers, the plants, the trees,—everything that met his eyes, was strange to him. And what was more, those who had begun the journey with him were now separated from him; some had remained behind, and some had died. Ever reflecting on the past, his heart was thoughtful and sad. Suddenly, while at the side of this jasper figure, he beheld a merchant presenting in homage to it a fan of white silk of the country of Tsin [*Fa Hian's own province in China.*] Without anyone perceiving it, this excited so great an emotion that the tears flowed and filled his eyes."

It is curious that, about twenty years after Fa Hian, another famous visitor should come to Lanka, and for a reason much like Fa Hian's. *Buddha-ghosa* was a learned young Brahman of North India who had a good knowledge of the religions and the religious disputes of his time, and who was fond of arguing about them. He went to various places in India discussing these matters with the learned men whom he found there. One day he came to a vihara (for Buddhism was still the religion of parts of North India) and there he was converted to Buddhism. He now became an earnest preacher of it, so eloquent and famous a preacher that to the people it seemed that the Buddha himself had come to earth again. They called him Buddha-ghosa, the *Voice of the Buddha.*

But in India there was no copy of the *Commentaries*, that is, the notes and explanations which were written to help the priests to understand the *Tri-pitaka* aright. Mahinda had taught the law of the Buddha orally to the priests in Lanka, and nearly two hundred years afterwards, Valagam Bahu had caused Mahinda's explanations to be put into writing in the Sinhalese language. Buddha-ghosa had shewn in India that he understood Buddhism; he had written one or two books on the subject. He now came to Lanka to copy the *Commentaries*, and to translate them back into the Pali language, the language in which Mahinda had taught them. Not till he had proved to them that he was qualified for this task did the Maha Vihara priests allow him to do as he wished. Buddha-ghosa did his work so well that his Pali translation is the one now used by the priests, while the Sinhalese book is forgotten, and no copy of it is to be found. Besides this translation, he wrote an entirely new book, the *Visuddhi Margaya*, which gives the whole of the Buddhist teachings in a short form.

After spending three years in Lanka, Buddha-ghosa returned to India, "to worship at the bo-tree" there. But he will always be remembered as the priest who explained the teachings of Buddhism in the way in which they are now taught in Lanka, in Burma, and in Siam.

XX.

THE STORY OF THE LION ROCK

As you leave Dambulla and go along the old road to Trincomalie, you now and again catch glimpses of a great brown rock some distance away, almost hidden by the thick jungle on all sides, but shewing itself when the windings of the road leave some open space. To get to it, you take a road branching off from the main road, and after a few miles you come on open ground, and suddenly the rock stands before you. On one side of it, and at its foot, lies a lake filled during the rains with clear, fresh water. Here and there you may find large stones which once formed part of a wall surrounding the rock. The land round about is all jungle now, but when the jungle is cleared we may find signs of houses, gardens, and temples that were here fourteen hundred years ago. The rock itself is high and has steep sides which no man can climb, but a narrow road winds round it to the top. On the rock you find the remains of old halls and stair-ways, and baths and cisterns for water. There is a cave which has painted on its walls a number of remarkable pictures, still clear and distinct, and these give us some idea of the dress and customs of the old times.

What is the story of *Sigiriya*, or *Sihagiriya*—for so the rock is named, from the carved figures of lions which you see as you toil upwards along the narrow road winding to the top of the rock?

The Tamils had again come to Lanka, and for about twenty-five years they reigned at Anuradhapura. Then, a Sinhalese prince named **Dhatu Sena**, who had been sheltered and educated as a priest by his uncle, the priest Mahanama, in the Ruhuna province, succeeded at last in driving out the Tamils and bringing the country again under a Sinhalese ruler. King Dhatu Sena reigned for eighteen years, and did all he could to restore Buddhism to its former glory, for the Tamils had done much harm to the sacred buildings and the old religion had been neglected by the Sinhalese who lived in and near the capital when the Tamils held it. Many of the leading men had even joined the Tamils, thinking it safe and profitable for them to be friendly with their conquerors. These were punished and degraded, quite rightly, by Dhatu Sena; while those who had loyally stood by him in his troubles were richly rewarded. The King repaired and much improved the great Brazen Palace which was in ruins, and other buildings. He built eighteen large viharas and tanks, besides eighteen smaller ones. But his grandest work was the *Kala-wewa*, a tank seven or eight square miles in extent. It is a hundred times larger than the Kandy Lake and nearly as large as the whole town of Colombo.

Another fact worth noting about Dhatu Sena is the respect he paid to the memory of

Mahinda, the priest who brought Buddhism into Lanka. He ordered an image of the priest to be made, and this was taken in procession to the place where Mahinda's body was burnt about two hundred years earlier. Here a great festival was held, and the *Dipa-vansa*, the oldest history of Lànka, was read aloud to all who were present. From this history and other old books, the priest Mahanama made up the book called the *Maha-vansa*, from which we get most of our information about the Sinhalese—about their coming to Lanka and how they settled in the island, about the bringing in of Buddhism and how this religion grew and flourished in Lanka. Mahanama could, of course, write the history only down to the time in which he lived; but after him others wrote of what happened in later times. It should be remembered that the *Maha-vansa* and all the great books on Buddhism were written, not in Sinhalese, but in the language called Pali, and in Pali verse.

But we must get back to Dhatu Sena who, in spite of all his good deeds, died a terrible death. He had two sons, Kasyapa and Mugalan, and these were step-brothers. Kasyapa's mother was a woman of lower rank than the king's, and **Kasyapa** saw that he could win the throne only by fighting for it. He got all the discontented and wicked men on his side, imprisoned his father, and so made himself king. Mugalan, seeing that nothing could be done at that time to save his father or himself, fled to India and tried to raise an army there.

Kasyapa next tried to get the riches which he was told his father had hidden away. He sent several messengers to Dhatu Sena asking him to say where the treasure was kept, but to all the messengers Dhatu Sena answered nothing. He knew that the requests were only part of a plot to kill him, for he had hidden no treasure, and he was prepared to die. He wished, however, to see his friend Mahanama once more, and to bathe in the Kala-wewa, before his enemies put him to death, and he thought of a plan by which he could get what he wanted.

The next time messengers came, he told them he would find the treasure if he was taken to the Kala-wewa. When he got there, and had spent some time in talk with Mahanama about religion, he bathed in the noble tank which he himself had built. Then turning to Kasyapa's servants he quietly said, "Friends, this is all the treasure I have."

Kasyapa was exceedingly angry when he heard these things, and he commanded that his father should be put to death. This he did not only because he was jealous of Mugalan for whom he thought his father was keeping the money, but also because so long as his father lived there was a danger that the people might restore him to the throne. Dhatu Sena was chained to the walls of a prison and the walls were built over him and plastered up with clay. So died this king.

There still remained a dangerous enemy who might at any time bring an army against Kasyapa. This was Mugalan, whose anger king Kasyapa dreaded, and whose return to Lanka was continually expected. Besides, how could the people be loyal to a ruler whose wickedness was known far and wide? Anuradhapura did not seem safe enough for him. "He took himself," says the *Maha-vansa*, "to the Sihagiri rock, that was hard for men to climb." Here he brought all the wealth he had collected, and buried it in various places. Here he built a splendid palace, furnished with everything that a king and his company could need for comfort and for enjoyment; and round the rock he built a strong wall by means of which he could defend himself from the attacks of his enemies. It is the ruins of the palace, the gardens, the houses, and the temples built by Kasyapa that we see to-day.

Anuradhapura, the capital, was not neglected. Kasyapa made it more beautiful than before by planting gardens at the gates, and by building additional viharas and alms-houses. He tried to please the priests by observing the sacred days, and to gain forgiveness for his evil deeds by performing ceremonies and penances, and by encouraging the priests to copy the sacred books. But no comfort came to him from these actions. On the contrary, he was filled with fear. He feared the world to come after death, for he had done great wrong; and in this world he had always the fear of Mugalan and his vengeance.

Mugalan came when Kasyapa had reigned for seventeen years, and a terrible fight took place at a village near Kurunegala between the step-brothers: "the two armies encountered each other like two seas that had burst their bounds." At a very important moment a fatal mistake was made. Kasyapa was going forward on his elephant and came to a marsh. He turned to go by another way. His army, however, thought that he was giving up the fight and was trying to escape from the field, and they too began to flee. Kasyapa saw that the battle was lost, and in despair he killed himself.

Mugalan now became king. He was very bitter against those who had joined Kasyapa and helped to put his father Dhatu Sena to death. It is said that in his rage he gnashed his teeth to such an extent that one tooth was permanently thrust out, and for that reason he was nicknamed the "*Rakshasa*," or demon, since demons were supposed to have two large teeth sticking out from the corners of their mouths. In time his anger cooled and he became a pious king.

Sigiriya was made a vihara and given to the priest Mahanama who had been Dhatu Sena's friend.

XXI.

THE KING WHO LOVED A POET

The king's name was **Kumara Dasa**. He was the son of King Mugalan, and he was himself a poet. One of his poems is about Rama and Sita, whose story is told at the beginning of this book. This poem is all that remains to us of his writings.

The poet whom the king loved was named *Kalidasa*. Kalidasa is said to have lived at Matara, where many Sinhalese poets and other famous men were born; but some think that he lived in a small town, (which no longer exists) near Kurunegala.

Very little is said about king Kumara Dasa in the old books. We are told that "his form was like unto a god, and he was a man of great strength." He was a just king and a well-known scholar. He was a strict Buddhist and "satisfied" the priests by giving them what they required. He purified Buddhism by calling the priests together and making them correct the mistakes that were found in copies of the sacred books. No doubt he built many tanks and viharas. It is a pity that so little is known about him, for he is believed to have been a strong as well as a wise ruler. He reigned only nine years, and might have reigned longer but for what happened to his friend Kalidasa.

There was a woman of the city whom the king used to visit frequently, for she was both beautiful and witty. On one of these visits he wrote two lines of verse on the wall of her house, and below these lines he added a promise to reward anyone who should complete the verse. The two lines written by the king were like an unfinished riddle, and any one who took up the king's challenge had not only to write a suitable answer, but also to write the answer in verse.

But the poet Kalidasa could do what a person of ordinary cleverness could not do. He found out the right answer and wrote it in verse on the wall above the king's lines. But he did not write his name, and the wicked woman who lived in the house resolved to get for herself the reward promised by the king. She secretly killed the poet, hid his body, and then went to the king and claimed the reward, saying it was she who had made up the answer. The king could not believe her, and enquiries were made. In the end the truth came out. The wicked woman was put to death and her body thrown into the river. Kalidasa's dead body was searched for, found, and then burned with every mark of honour. The king was bitterly grieved at the loss of his friend. So great was his sorrow that when the poet's body was burning on the funeral pile, he and six of his queens threw themselves into the flame and so died.

There is a pretty story told, that seven bo-trees sprang from the ground at the spot where this burning took place, to represent the king and his six queens. Hence the place is called *Hath-bodiya-watte*, the garden of the seven bo-trees, and one of these trees is believed to be still in existence. But it is uncertain whether the garden is the one at Anuradhapura or the one at Matara.

XXII.

THE FALL OF ANURADHAPURA

For five hundred years after the death of king Kumara Dasa the history of Lanka is a story of disorder, strife, and bloodshed. Now and again a strong king would arise who kept the country in order and crushed the attempts of bold, bad men to create mischief and to stir rebellion. Then the religion of the people would be encouraged and their priests honoured. Great festivals would be celebrated with proper ceremony and the relics carried through crowded streets in solemn processions. Learning would be given the respect due to it. Poets would flourish under the king's favour, books on religion would be composed, and the three *Pitakas* would be publicly read for the instruction of the pious. Under such kings, life and property would be safe, and both king and people would be able to "take their pleasure heartily."

But such kings were rare, and the death of each was followed by disputes for the throne and much fighting. A son would plot against his father, a brother against his brother, a servant against his lord. There were always rivals who claimed the throne, and each was sure of a number of followers. In their quarrels these rival chiefs would plunder and lay waste any district where the people were not in their favour. The land was thus ruined. The cultivation of rice was neglected. The rich oppressed the poor, and the strong persecuted the weak. The temples were robbed of their treasures. It is true that whoever became king began at once to offer gifts to the priests, to build tanks and viharas, and to repair the broken temples. But the country suffered by these continual wars, and everywhere there was poverty, distrust, and confusion. A good many of the kings during these years reigned for not more than three years each, and some reigned only for a few days.

Much of this disorder was due to the Tamils, who soon discovered how weak the Sinhalese people had become. We begin to hear again of these Tamils about a hundred years after the death of Kumara Dasa, when one of the Sinhalese princes who wished to become king of Lanka went over to India and brought to Lanka a Tamil army. He was defeated, and his Tamil soldiers were given as slaves to various viharas. But other Sinhalese princes also brought armies from India, and generally succeeded in winning and wearing the crown of Lanka for a time. Still, the Tamils had to be paid for their services, and when the new king had no money the soldiers were evidently allowed to pay themselves by what they could get by plundering the temples and the people. But this was not all. The kings themselves would plunder the vihara and dagobas. The images and coverings of gold were melted down and the gold was taken; the offerings were taken; the gems which pious worshippers gave to ornament the sacred statues were taken; and in this way the Tamils were paid. Little by little the Tamils became very powerful in Lanka, though sometimes a Sinhalese king would be strong enough to keep them down; but the kings found out too late that they had gone too far in getting help from outside, and that it was a mistake to bring the Tamils into the island.

The capital, Anuradhapura, already stripped of its riches, became now unsafe for the king to live in, and he looked for a city farther away from the Tamils. **Agbo IV**. who kept the Tamils in check to some extent, found it safer towards the close of his reign, to remove to *Polonnaruwa*, fifty miles south-east of Anuradhapura, and here, indeed, he died. On his death a Tamil named *Pottha-kuttha* was so powerful that he was able to choose two persons, one after the other, to be kings of Lanka in name, while he himself held the real power. A hundred years after Agbo IV, Polonnaruwa became the capital of Lanka under **Sena I.** This was about the year 846 A. D., and Polonnaruwa continued to be the capital for four hundred and fifty years after, though sometimes other places, and even Anuradhapura, had the honour of being the king's chief town.

But never again was Anuradhapura so glorious as it was in those old days, when kings were glad and anxious to give their thought, their time, and their money, freely, to make it a city worthy of a rich and pious people, a city worthy of the gods. Here Mahinda and Sangamitta preached, and here they died. Here Devanampiya Tissa enshrined the first relics of the Buddha, and established the religion which to this day counts so many millions of followers in Lanka and in other lands. Here the Maha Vihara with its spacious gardens and quiet shades sheltered and instructed the priests of Buddhism. Here Dutu-Gemunu built the Lowa Maha Paya and the Maha Thupa. Here reigned the kings of the Great Dynasty; and here came travellers from countries far and near, to see the wonders and learn the teachings of which they had heard in their own land

They call Anuradhapura a "Buried City," a "City of the Dead." For hundreds of years its shrines and temples have been neglected, and sand and jungle have covered its ruins. But the city is *not* dead. Its very ruins call aloud to every true son of Lanka, reminding him of its past greatness, and bidding him live and work for the good of his people and his country.

XXIII.

VIJAYA BAHU

After some time, even Polonnaruwa was not safe from the Tamils who swarmed into the country and did very much as they pleased. One king, Mahinda V., who kept a Tamil army in his service, found that he could get no money from his own people to pay the soldiers. The Tamil soldiers began to press him for their pay and he fled secretly from them into Ruhuna, where he reigned undisturbed for many years. When the news of this reached the king of Chola, in India, a large army of Tamils was sent to Lanka, and the king and queen were taken prisoners and sent to India with all the royal treasures. Then, a Tamil chief ruled at Polonnaruwa, while in Ruhuna the Sinhalese still had some power, though Sinhalese princes who were strong enough to make themselves kings once moved their capital to Kalutara, and at another time to Kataragama.

Meanwhile, a young prince was growing up who made it his object to free his country not only from the Tamils but also from those Sinhalese chiefs who were wrongly claiming the royal power. He began his task in Ruhuna where, when he was only sixteen years old, he won a battle (at Kataragama) against the chief who ruled Ruhuna. In a short time he made all the chiefs in that district acknowledge him as the rightful king of Lanka. He took the title of **Vijaya Bahu** and was the first of that name.

Having set in order his own district, he planned an attack on the Tamils. But Vijaya Bahu's doings in Ruhuna had already come to the ears of the Tamil chief at Polonnaruwa, who sent an army to Kataragama to put down the daring prince. Vijaya Bahu saw that the Tamil army was too strong for him to fight at that time. He wisely took refuge in a hill fort where the Tamils could not follow him, and the latter had to go back after laying waste the country round Kataragama.

Then Vijaya sent messengers to the Buddhist king of Burma, asking him for help. The Burmese could not send soldiers, but they sent large quantities of cloths of different kinds. with other valuable gifts, such as camphor and sandal-wood. These gifts helped the king to reward his own soldiers.

The feeling against the Tamils spread widely among the Sinhalese and soon the people of Anuradhapura and the surrounding districts were divided in opinion. Some of them were in favour of the Tamils, either through fear, or because they were comfortable enough though a Tamil chief governed them. But others were ashamed to be under the rule of their old enemies, and they believed that Vijaya Bahu was able to make them again a free and independent nation. These patriots began the war by refusing to pay the taxes which the Tamils demanded, and they insulted the officers who came to collect the taxes. The Tamil king in Chola sent an army to punish these bold men, and in all the districts where the Tamils were strong the Sinhalese were subdued. Then the Tamils marched slowly to Ruhuna, which was to them the most troublesome part of the Island. They were a mighty host, and spread over the country, "like unto a sea that had burst its bounds." Two of Vijaya Bahu's captains were terrified and soon submitted to the Tamil general, turning against their own king and people. But after a fierce battle, Vijaya Bahu defeated the Tamils and killed their general. This success was a great encouragement to the Sinhalese, and they begged the king to take advantage of his victory: "Now is the time for thee, O king, to go to the city of Polonnaruwa."

The Tamil king of Chola in India was so angry when he heard of Vijaya Bahu's success, that he sent another army, larger than the former ones, to punish the Sinhalese and to make their king a prisoner. This army won some victories at the start, and the king had to retire from Anuradhapura and Polonnaruwa to his rock fortresses, where for three months he held out against the enemy. A rebellion among some of his own people then gave him trouble for some time; but when that was put down, he sent four armies to attack the Tamils from two different directions. These troops succeeded so well that the king was able to collect all his forces and march towards Polonnaruwa. The two chiefs who had before turned against him now came back, and helped him in the attack on Polonnaruwa where the Tamil forces were gathered. After a long siege the city was taken and the power of the Tamils was destroyed. Vijaya Bahu entered Anuradhapura in triumph, "and the king of the Cholians having heard of the destruction of his hosts, sent not any more men to Lanka, saying, 'Now are the Sinhalese powerful.'"

But Lanka had suffered so much from the attacks of the Tamils that Vijaya Bahu had a difficult task when he tried to set things in order. To prevent any dissatisfaction among the people he ordered that the taxes should be collected according to the means of the people, and that the magistrates should decide matters justly in courts of law. The poor were given food; cripples were allowed bulls for their use; the lame and the blind had lands set apart for them, from the profit of which they were supported; "and out of his great compassion he gave rice for ravens, and dogs, and other beasts."

The low state into which Buddhism had fallen may be understood when we read that not even ten well-behaved priests could be found in Lanka: so fully had the Tamils succeeded in their attempts to destroy the religion of the Sinhalese people. Vijaya Bahu sent to Burma for pious and virtuous priests, and these ordained as many others as were necessary for Lanka. Then Buddhism was again prosperous. Many rich gifts of viharas and lands were made to the priests. The path to the top of Adam's Peak was cleared, and pilgrims to that shrine were provided with resting-places and with food. The old festivals were celebrated anew. The sacred writings were regularly read to the people, and copies of them were made for the priests. The king himself translated one of the books into Sinhalese, spending every morning in his room and allowing no one to disturb him in his work.

These reforms did not please everybody, and more than once the king had to fight to keep his power. Four years after he entered Anuradhapura, some of his chief ministers in Ruhuna rebelled against him, and he had to take an army to that province and make the people obey him again. A few years later, the king of the Cholians insulted the messengers sent to him by Vijaya Bahu. An army, consisting partly of Tamils, was prepared to attack Chola; but the Tamils rebelled and plundered Polonnaruwa. Again Vijaya Bahu was forced to fight, and he defeated the rebels, punishing them severely.

Vijaya Bahu reigned fifty-five years. It is interesting to notice that he was not only a great king and soldier, but also a poet, and liberal in his gifts to deserving scholars.

XXIV.

A PRINCE OF RUHUNA

When Vijaya died there was again trouble in Lanka. First of all, his son **Vikrama Bahu I** had to fight no fewer than six battles against his own relations, before he could become king at Polonnaruwa. Even then he had no power in Ruhuna, where three of his cousins ruled over three divisions of that district. Thus there were "four lords of the land" in Lanka, and the object of each was to get as much plunder as he could from his unfortunate people. "Even as the mill extracts juice from the sugar-cane," so did these four lords oppress their subjects.

But king Vikrama Bahu of Polonnaruwa was the worst of the four. He employed "strangers" (Tamils, most likely) to fight for him, and paid them with plunder taken from the Buddhist viharas. Some of the priests had helped his relatives to fight against him, and he could not forget that. He treated the priests with great cruelty, robbing them of their offerings, their treasures, their relics, and their viharas, so that they were forced to leave the king's country for Ruhuna, staying wherever the people were willing to give them shelter. Families of high rank found it was safer to take themselves away to places where they were not so well known, and where there was less danger of oppression. Also, the soldiers of the four kings quarrelled among themselves and fought continually, burning villages in their rage, breaking open the tanks, cutting down coconut palms and other useful trees. Servants refused to obey their masters, labourers armed themselves and went out in companies to plunder the villages and to rob on the highways. The people who lived farthest away from the chief towns refused to pay taxes and openly broke the law. So bad was the condition of things "that it might be said of the whole country of Lanka, from north to south, and from east to west, 'They who love ruin and destruction are wandering over the land'."

Things were no better when Vikrama Bahu I died after a reign of twenty-one years, and his son **Gaja Bahu II** became king at Polonnaruwa. Very different was this second Gaja Bahu from the first king of that name. The first was a warrior and a leader of his people. The second was a weak ruler of whom his own father said, "He can neither get what he has not, nor keep that which he has."

But a new deliverer was soon to shew himself in Lanka, who in time freed his country from the enemies who plagued it like thorns, who established order and caused the laws to be obeyed, who made the people contented and prosperous, who restored religion, and who was to prove himself one of the greatest of the kings of Lanka—as pious a king as Devanampiya Tissa, as brave as the valiant Dutu-Gemunu.

This new hero was **Parakrama Bahu**, the son of one of the three lords of Ruhuna, and a cousin of king Gaja Bahu II.

Parakrama was born not very far from the present town of Badulla, in a village now called Alupota. The astrologers in his father's house foretold that he would be a very fortunate prince, able to subdue not only the whole of Lanka, but also the whole of India. He was carefully brought up in Ruhuna, and was taught all that a great prince was expected to know. He learnt grammar, poetry, and music. He was instructed in the laws of Buddhism. He was trained to ride, to hunt, and to use both the sword and the bow. Even more, his mind was filled with stories of the brave deeds of Rama and the Buddha and other valiant heroes of the old time, and he burned to follow their example.

Parakrama was not satisfied to remain a petty king in his own little district. He wished to be powerful and famous. He was vexed to think that though Lanka was so small an island, yet it was divided among so many rulers, each of whom was like a "village headman," caring for nothing more than to govern his own portion of the country. This prince of Ruhuna had a prouder spirit. He would bring all the people under his own rule, and restore to Lanka its ancient greatness and prosperity.

XXV.

PARAKRAMA VISITS POLONNARUWA

There were two ways which Parakrama might have tried to gain his object and become sole king of all Lanka. He might first have made himself master of Ruhuna, and then gone on to win the throne of Polonnaruwa, for this throne was considered the greatest, and he who reigned at Polonnaruwa was the true king of all the Sinhalese. Or, Parakrama might first conquer Polonnaruwa, and then easily bring the smaller district of Ruhuna under his rule. The second was the more daring plan, and he chose it because he thought that if he once became king of Ruhuna he would then be too comfortable to think of a difficult war against Polonnaruwa. He too would be satisfied to remain a "village headman."

Before, however, he could undertake the great war he had in mind, there were some things to be done. He must get together a number of followers whom he could train, and on whom he could depend. He must know how many soldiers Gaja Bahu had, and how much money and grain he had stored up. He must know how the people in the Raja-Rata liked their king, and if they could be made to rebel against him. All this information

Parakrama must himself find out, and it must be found out without making Gaja Bahu suspicious. For this purpose he determined to make a visit to Polonnaruwa.

His father was now dead, and the young prince lived under the care of his uncle Kitsirime, one of the two remaining lords of Ruhuna. As soon as a convenient opportunity came, Parakrama stole secretly out of the palace by night, escaped the guards who watched the roads, and met his followers at an appointed place not far from Badulla. He was disappointed to find that there were not so many men present as he expected, and even the few who came were timid and half-hearted, for they knew that by taking part in this adventure they were in fact rebelling against their king. But Parakrama was not to be turned back. His own boldness and the hopeful words he spoke encouraged his men, and they went willingly on till they came to Badulla, which was then only a village. Here they found Sangha, a general who had been appointed governor of the district by Kitsirime. Sangha received the prince with proper respect and shewed him and his followers much kindness. But he soon suspected there was something wrong, and that king Kitsirime did not know about the prince's journey. Like a loyal subject he sent word to the king, and meanwhile detained the prince. This was awkward for Parakrama, and there was no way out of the difficulty but by ordering his men to kill Sangha. The general's soldiers and the people of his district rose in arms against the visitors, but Parakrama boldly met the angry crowd and put an end to their uproar. After all, he was a prince, and the people were not unwilling to take him for their leader. Indeed, in a few days the people from the surrounding districts came to him and said they were ready to support him if he wished to fight against Kitsirime. They naturally thought that Parakrama wanted only to be king of Ruhuna.

This was not Parakrama's intention. We know that he wanted to go to Polonnaruwa and spy out that kingdom. Leaving Badulla, he pushed on to the north. Twice he escaped being killed by those who were faithful to Kitsirime. Then Kitsirime himself began to fear that the prince was plotting against him, and that if he did not prevent it his people would leave him and join the prince. But all the armies sent by Kitsirime were unsuccessful in their attempts to capture the prince, who pushed on and at length came to a village belonging to the kingdom of Gaja Bahu.

King Gaja Bahu was not pleased to hear that his cousin was so near him. He had heard of what Parakrama had done all the way from Ruhuna, and he was anxious as to what might now happen in his own kingdom. He called his ministers together and they talked about what was best to be done. At last they decided that it would not be wise to offend Parakrama. They would receive him as a friendly prince, treat him well, and pretend to believe that he had come because he was not satisfied with

Kitsirime. Rich gifts were sent to Parakrama by messengers who welcomed him to Polonnaruwa, and Gaja Bahu himself went out to meet him, and bring him with all possible honour into the capital.

But Parakrama did not forget why he had come. He lived in Gaja Bahu's palace and made himself very agreeable to the king. He sent for his sister and married her to the king; this made the king trust him entirely. He went about the streets with a spirited elephant and pretending that he was chased by it, he would run into the houses of men of high rank, and win their friendship with suitable gifts, Pretending that he was only amusing himself by hunting, he went from place to place, and found out how the guards were stationed in the city. He talked freely to all the people he met, and thus knew each man's character, while by his gifts and his familiar ways he made himself exceedingly popular with them.

His men were not idle. The prince secretly sent out those whom he could trust to spy out the country, to get all the information they could, and to make the people discontented with Gaja Bahu. These men did their business well. They disguised themselves in various ways, some as snake-dancers, some as musicians, others as traders, as begging monks, as pilgrims, and as physicians. Some were received in people's houses as religious teachers. All these men cleverly made the people trust them, and little by little taught them to dislike Gaja Bahu.

Whatever information was obtained was carefully written down, and Parakrama soon knew more about the Raja-Rata than king Gaja Bahu himself.

XXVI.

PARAKRAMA AND THE WAR

This friendship between king Gaja Bahu and Parakrama could not last very long. Parakrama was deceiving the king and was no true friend to him. He was setting up the people against the king and this was sure to be found out and to bring about trouble at some time. But the friendship was broken off through the king's jealousy. He did not like his subjects to be too fond of the young stranger, as that meant danger to his own throne.

One day, Parakrama did a bold deed which made the people admire and praise him more than ever. He was being carried in his palanquin through the town when a savage buffalo was seen dashing along the road, killing and wounding all who came in its way. The palanquin-bearers and all the prince's attendants fled in terror. But the prince was too proud to shew fear. He bravely faced the fierce beast and shouted at it, on which the bull stopped for a moment, then turned and fled. "And they who saw this marvel with their own eyes, and they who heard thereof, were astonished, and praised him loudly."

When the Prince saw that Gaja Bahu was jealous of him, he left Polonnaruwa and returned to Ruhuna, where he was warmly welcomed back by Kitsirime who was now an old man. Parakrama had learnt all he wanted to know, and had himself seen the state of the northern kingdom. Not long after his return, Kitsirime died, and Parakrama succeeded him as governor or king of part of Ruhuna. The time had now come for him to make ready for a great war against Gaja Bahu. He would begin by putting things in order in his own kingdom.

To keep Ruhuna safe from the attacks of enemies he placed companies of soldiers as guards at different places all the way from Adam's Peak to the sea-coast. Next, he began to heap up vast stores of grain, and to encourage the cultivation of paddy. So anxious was Parakrama to make the land rich and fruitful, chiefly in rice-fields, that he declared that not the smallest space of ground in his kingdom should lie unused, not a drop of rain should flow through his rivers without first profiting his people. Thus large tracts of rice-fields, and groves of fruit-bearing trees, and gardens of sweet-smelling flowers took the place of wild, uncultivated ground. Ponds were made for pleasant bathing. Old tanks were cleared of weed and jungle, while very many new tanks were built in places where they would be found useful. Some of the tanks got their water from rivers with which they were connected by canals. Other tanks were formed by building dams across streams and rivers. One tank was of such exceeding size and beauty that it was known as the "Sea of Parakrama."

Without an ample supply of both money and soldiers it was impossible to carry on a war; but the people had long been heavily taxed and the prince did not wish them to suffer more by having to pay too much. He decided that his generals were no longer to collect the taxes. Separate ministers were appointed for this purpose, and they had also to keep proper accounts of all the money collected by taxes and in other ways. A good deal was got by selling to other countries the gems obtained from the Ratnapura district. Doubtless paddy was sold, and the rent of the king's lands must have brought in large sums.

Much trouble was taken to get together both a sufficient store of materials for war and a large number of fighting men. Thousands of soldiers were enrolled and armed in every district, and regiments of Tamils and probably of Veddas were formed. The children of well-born families were taken into Parakrama's palace and there taught the art of war, different languages, music, dancing, and all things that would make them useful in the service of the king. Mock battles were often fought in the streets of Polonnaruwa to accustom the soldiers to the practice of war.

The only thing now wanted was an excuse

to begin the war. This excuse was soon found. Gaja Bahu had invited a number of foreign princes to Polonnaruwa, and Parakrama was displeased that this was done. He feared that one of these princes might be chosen, on Gaja Bahu's death, to succeed him as King. Besides, these princes were not Buddhists, and Buddhism would not be helped by them. Parakrama gave orders, therefore, to begin the attack on the king's country.

The whole plan of the war was first carefully arranged, and was as carefully carried out. Parakrama's generals won battle after battle on their march northward, and slowly fought their way to Anuradhapura. Then came the advance to Polonnaruwa. The spies, whom Parakrama had left behind in the city when he left it, now opened the gates to his officers, and Gaja Bahu was captured and kept a prisoner in his own palace. Contrary to Parakrama's orders, the victorious soldiers plundered the city and behaved so badly that the people begged Manabharana (who ruled another part of Ruhuna) to come to their assistance. His army and Gaja Bahu's utterly defeated the invaders, and then Manabharana shewed what sort of a man he was. He wanted the crown for himself and tried to kill king Gaja Bahu by starvation and poison. The king sent messengers to Parakrama to ask for help, and help was readily given. Manabharana was defeated and Gaja Bahu set at liberty. Then the priests came to Parakrama who naturally expected to be made king. They pointed out that Gaja

Bahu was too ill to live long and that he had no son to succeed him ; Parakrama could therefore wait a little. It was a great thing that the priests asked, but Parakrama generously gave way. He obeyed them and returned to Ruhuna, leaving Gaja Bahu on the throne.

XXVII.

PARAKRAMA'S UMBRELLA

When Gaja Bahu again reigned at Polonnaruwa Manabharana sent him gifts and proposed that they should join together to put down the power of Parakrama. But Gaja Bahu would not consent ; he was determined to be faithful to the agreement he had made with the prince who had given him back his kingdom. To make the matter more sure, he went to a vihara and there he publicly made this solemn statement : "*I have given Raja-Rata to King Parakrama.*" This meant that on his death the throne should go to Parakrama and no one else. He ordered that the words he had spoken should be inscribed on a stone and then he returned home, where he died not long afterwards.

Manabharana made one more attempt to win the great prize of the kingdom of Lanka, and some of Gaja Bahu's ministers were foolish enough to help him against Parakrama. Many fierce battles were the result. Parakrama was now very angry. He vowed that he would not give Manabharana a resting-place even in Ruhuna; and he did not. Manabharana's armies were utterly defeated; the whole of Ruhuna was conquered, and Parakrama then came to Polonnaruwa as sole king of Lanka. Thousands of his people met him on the way and brought him to his palace with loud rejoicing. Arches gay with flags and flowers lined the crowded streets. The noise of the drums was like the roaring of the ocean in stormy weather. Elephants clad in cloth of gold dazzled the eyes of the lookers-on. The sounds of songs of praise and welcome mingled with the shouting, the clapping of hands, and the cheers of the multitude, "Live! O Live, Great King!"

Well might the king be proud as he entered the city. He had gained the high end for which he had worked from his youth. He was now no "village headman." He had brought every part of the island under his "umbrella of dominion,"—for, as an umbrella covers and protects those beneath it so did the king guard and govern all his subjects.

It was now Parakrama's task as king to correct all that was badly done in the country and to improve his people in every possible way. He gave orders that the taxes should be fairly laid upon the people without being a burden to them, and at the same time without loss to the king's revenue. The great families that had been ruined and had fled from the oppression of former kings, were called back and restored to their former positions. Arrangements were made for the proper support of the poor. Hospitals were built, and carefully-trained physicians were appointed to attend to the sick. Order was established everywhere and the laws were well obeyed; so well, that even a woman carrying with her a costly jewel might travel anywhere in the island and no one would dare so much as to ask her what it was.

The king was a devout Buddhist, and part of his plan was to make Buddhism again the chief care of his people. He had been thoroughly taught the laws and the teachings of his religion. But the condition of Buddhism at that time pained him much. The priests were most of them quite careless about their duties. They thought only of making themselves comfortable and forgot the vows they had made when they became priests. The three chief Orders, or societies, of priests—those belonging to the Maha vihara, the Abhayagiri vihara, and the Jetavana vihara—had for eight hundred years been separated from one another and had become unfriendly. The king took great trouble to unite the three brotherhoods and he succeeded at last. The careless priests in all the viharas were disrobed and given other employment. Then, as the people began to pay more attention to their religion, viharas were built or repaired, images of the Buddha were set up, and new preaching halls provided in many places.

Parakrama continued to do throughout his whole kingdom of Lanka what he had done before in Ruhuna for the cultivation of rice. Tanks—over a thousand of them—were repaired or newly built to provide an unfailing supply of water for the wants of the people, and these tanks were in many cases joined by canals to rivers and large streams. We have already heard of the "Sea of Parakrama." This name is also given to a number of tanks—Minneriya, Kantalai, and others—which were connected by a canal a hundred miles long, starting from the Amba Ganga at Ellahara near Matale.

The old books tell us much about the improvements made by Parakrama to Polonnaruwa and Anuradhapura; about the fine roads, the gardens, the palaces, and the new cities that he built. But we have still to do with the king's enemies who were as busy as ever both within and outside his kingdom.

There were two rebellions in Ruhuna. Some of the chiefs there made queen Sugali (Manabharana's mother) believe that her kingdom was strong enough to be independent of Parakrama. She made ready for war. Parakrama "smiled sweetly" when he heard of this and ordered his generals to put out the wild fire of this rebellion with showers of arrows. But it took a long time, and it cost the lives of thousands of brave men before the fire was quenched. Queen Sugali was at last made prisoner and her armies were utterly defeated. The tooth-relic and the bowl-relic were taken from her charge, and a splendid Feast of Lights was celebrated in the capital in honour of the event. The second rebellion in Ruhuna was a smaller affair.

So great a warrior was Parakrama that he did not fear to carry on a war even beyond the seas which surround Lanka. There was an old friendship, as we know, between the kings of Lanka and Aramana in Burma, both countries being Buddhist in religion. But the enemies of Parakrama carried false tales to Aramana, and the king of that country changed his friendship into enmity. He insulted Parakrama's messengers; he stopped the sale of his elephants to Lanka; he forbade Sinhalese ships to visit or trade with Burma; and one day he made prisoner a princess whom Parakrama had sent from Lanka to the King of Cambodia.

A Tamil general, named *Adhikari*, was sent with a large army to punish the king of Aramana. He was entirely successful. The king was taken and slain, and the Sinhalese entered his capital in triumph. Parakrama was declared supreme lord of Aramana, and a certain number of elephants had to be sent to him every year as a sign of his lordship over Aramana.

Then came war in Southern India. The king of Chola invaded Pandya and slew its king who had asked Parakrama for help. Parakrama sent his general *Lankapura* to Madura and the Cholians were driven out of the city, some of them being sent as prisoners to Lanka to repair the Ruanveli dagaba and other buildings that formerly the Tamils from Chola had destroyed.

Lankapura was not satisfied with his success in Pandya. He came to Rameswaram and after fighting five battles made the district a province of Ceylon. Then he went over to Chola and fought several battles there. That country too was made subject to Lanka, and money was coined there with the name of Parakrama as king of Chola.

XXVIII.

MAGHA OF KALINGA*

The Great Parakrama had made Lanka prosperous, and some of the kings who came after him tried to keep up the greatness to which the country had reached. **Vijaya Bahu II**, Parakrama's nephew and successor, is called a wise and prudent king because he took care not to stir up any bad feeling among the people, and because he pleased them by his kind acts. He set free those whom Parakrama had harshly imprisoned, and restored to them their lands and possessions. He added to the beauty and grandeur of the capital, Polonnaruwa. He won the friendship of the king of Aramana by writing to him "with his own hand, in the Pali tongue, a letter of great merit." He thus made the priests and people of the two countries—both

* Kalinga is the district in Eastern India now known as Orissa, or the district between the Mahanadi and the Godaveri rivers.

Buddhist countries—friendly again. But this wise king reigned only one year when he was meanly killed by a false friend, who in turn was killed after a reign of only five days.

Then reigned a king, **Kirti Nissanka Malla**, whose name is often found in the stone inscriptions he set up in various parts of the island. He belonged to the race of Kalinga, the district of India, from which, as we have learnt before, the tooth-relic was brought to Ceylon. He appears to have been a notable ruler, and a huge stone lion on which his throne was placed was brought from Polonnaruwa to Colombo a few years ago, and it may now be seen in the Colombo Museum.

But there is a difficulty in deciding as to how much this king actually did, for some of the things said to have been done by him are also said to have been done by Parakrama the Great. For example, he is said to have sent armies to fight against the kings of Chola and Pandya, to have brought all Lanka under one umbrella, to have reconciled the priests of the three Viharas, to have repaired certain tanks, and to have freed the country of robbers so that a woman could safely travel anywhere with her jewels.

Still, there were some deeds which perhaps were entirely done by Nissanka Malla himself. He rebuilt the famous Dambulla vihara and placed in it seventy-three images of the Buddha. He made some additions to the Ruanveli dagaba and built at Polonnaruwa a beautiful temple for the tooth-relic. To relieve the sufferings of the people he took no taxes from them for five years, and even gave lands and money to the very poor. He went round the country enquiring how the work of government was carried on, and held *durbars* of chiefs and officials to get their opinion on public matters. He was so devoted a Buddhist that he went in state with the four divisions of his army to the shrine of Adam's Peak to worship there.

Not twenty years after his death came **Magha**, a prince of Kalinga, with a huge army of 20,000 men. For twenty-one years Magha and his Kalingas ruled at Polonnaruwa doing all the mischief they could to the people and their cities, turning Lanka "into a house on fire." The description of their savage doings is well described in the *Mahavansa* :—

"Thereupon these mighty men, wicked disturbers of the peace of mankind, stalked about the land hither and thither crying out boastfully, 'Lo! we are the giants of Kerala.'* And they robbed the inhabitants of their garments and their jewels and everything that they had............They cut off also the hands and feet of the people, and despoiled their dwellings. Their oxen and buffaloes also, and other beasts, they bound up and carried them away forcibly. The rich men they tied up with cords and tortured, and took possession of all their wealth, and brought them to poverty. They broke down the image-houses and destroyed

* The Carnatic country, South-East coast of India.

many cetiyas.* They took up their dwellings in the viharas and beat the pious laymen therein. They flogged children, and sorely distressed the five ranks of the religious orders. They compelled the people to carry burdens and made them labour heavily. Many books also of great excellence did they loose from the cords that bound them and cast away in divers places. Even the great and lofty cetiyas, such as the Ratanavali [Ruanveli] which stood like the embodiment of the glory of all the pious kings of old, they spared not, but utterly destroyed them, and caused a great many bodily relics to disappear thereby, which were unto them as their lives. Alas! Alas!"

XXIX.

A SECOND PARAKRAMA

When Magha of Kalinga ruled in the north, and cruelly oppressed the Sinhalese of Rajarata, there were still Sinhalese princes who were strong enough to keep him away from the hill forts and districts where they still ruled over their own people. One of these little capitals was *Yapahu*, thirty-two miles north-east of Kurunegala, which later on became the capital of Lanka but of which only the ruins now remain. Another was

* Dagabas.

Dambadeniya, twenty-seven miles south-west of Kurunegala, where **Vijaya Bahu III** ruled as king, driving away the Tamils, settling disputes among the Buddhists, and trying to preserve the religion of the land.

But Vijaya Bahu's son, **Parakrama Bahu II**, did more for Lanka, He was a very learned prince, so learned that he came to be called "the all-knowing Pandit." He translated into Sinhalese the *Visuddhi-Margxya* which Buddha-ghosa had written in Pali eight hundred years before, and he wrote several poems of his own. He encouraged learning in every way. He brought priests and books from India, and required that the priests in Lanka should be well taught not only in all religious subjects but in grammar and other sciences as well. During his reign a priest wrote for the use of his brethren a valuable book on medicine which was translated into the languages of Cambodia, Siam, and Burma; and another priest wrote additional chapters to the book called the *Mahavansa*.

The second Parakrama was not a scholar only: he was also a great ruler. By his laws and the wise counsel he gave, order was established in the three Sinhalese *Ratas* or provinces, and his people had more peace than they had enjoyed for many years.

The Tamils who were at Polonnaruwa were alarmed when they heard of the Sinhalese king's success. Parakrama was continually thinking of the brave deeds of Dutu-Gemunu and Valagam Bahu when they delivered Lanka from the rule of the Tamils, and he made haste to follow their example. War soon began. The Sinhalese and Tamil armies met at the Kala-wewa and there a fierce battle was fought in which the Tamils were utterly defeated. All the plunder they had collected during the time they were in power was now taken away from them, and the few Tamils who escaped from the fight were glad enough to get away with their lives.

Then came to Lanka a Malay prince named *Chandra-bhanu* with a fierce band of Malay followers. As the Malays were then Buddhists in religion the Sinhalese received them kindly, but they soon tried to conquer the country and annoy the Sinhalese. There must have been a large number of them for they are said to have landed at different places, and to have wasted the land with "the fury of a flood of water." Vira Bahu, the king's nephew, was sent against them, and he drove them out of Lanka in spite of the poisoned arrows which they used in fighting. Chandra-bhanu fled to India, got together a host of Pandyans and Cholians, and came again, only to be again defeated.

These were all the king's wars. It was necessary he should fight, but having thus cleared Lanka of the enemies that pressed upon her like thorns, he turned his attention to the important works of peace. As we have seen, he did much to improve the condition of the priests; but much more had to be done if Buddhism was to be raised from the low condition into which it had fallen. All over the country neglected and ruined dagabas had to be repaired or rebuilt, officers had to be appointed to look after them, and the regular observance of the feasts and religious services had to be arranged. From Kurunegala to Dondra the ministers of Parakrama went about this task. The ruins of Anuradhapura were cleared of the jungle that had grown over them, and the famous dagabas in that city were repaired. Polonnaruwa, which had been badly plundered and spoiled by the Tamils, was restored to its former grandeur. and the king was crowned for the second time in that noble capital. The road to Adam's Peak was put into good order and, like other kings, this second Parakrama went there with his army to worship at the shrine of the foot-print.

Dambadeniya, the new capital, was naturally given much attention. Besides making the city beautiful with mansions and lofty walls and gates, he repaired the three-storeyed house of the tooth-relic, and held a seven-days feast in honour of the Buddha and the Buddhist religion. At Nambambaraya, the king's birthplace, a few miles distant from Dambadeniya, he built a great vihara to which the tooth-relic was conveyed in one of the grandest processions seen in Lanka. But more remarkable is the large number of bridges which Parakrama caused to be built, not only in the low-country, at places like Bentota and Kalutara, but even at Gampola, Ulapane, and Ambagamuwa in the hill districts.

XXX.

THE CITY OF VICTORY.

The sixty years which followed the death of Parakrama Bahu II were again times of confusion and disorder in Lanka. The Tamils in the north of the island had by this time established a kingdom of their own with Jaffna as its capital, and they now tried to bring the whole island under their rule. In this they were readily helped by the Pandyans, who sometimes came with their armies against Lanka on their own account as well. The Sinhalese were given no rest and their kings had to move from one place to another to be more safe from invasion. Within twenty years of Parakrama Bahu II's death, the famous city of Polonnaruwa ceased to be the capital of the Sinhalese, and even during those twenty years the king lived some years at Yapahu. After Polonnaruwa, Kurunegala became the chief city, and when **Vikrama Bahu III** was king, the "delightful" river-city, Gampola, was his capital.

In this king's reign a powerful chief lived in the "beautiful and famous" city of Peradeniya. His name was **Alakeswara**, or *Alagakkonara*, and for about forty years he was the chief man in Lanka, whom the people looked upon as their champion against the Tamils, and whose advice the kings held in the highest respect. It is not easy to find out the exact truth about much of his life, for those who have written about him do not all agree in their statements.

Vikrama Bahu III is called a "wise" king, but he was perhaps more "learned" than wise. He gave his attention to books chiefly, and left the management of his kingdom to Alakesvara whom he created *prabhu-raja* or viceroy. When he received his appointment he went down to Rayigama, where his family had settled, and strongly fortified that place, so that in times of danger the king could always have a place of safety. Then he began to build a new fort on the west coast.

The place selected was about four miles from Colombo. A steep high wall of stone was built round the new city which was further protected by a deep and broad ditch. A number of dams were built at various places to keep back the water, and, if necessary when enemies attacked the city, to let it out and flood the surrounding country. The city was adorned with gates, towers, and temples. The people who lived in it were many and prosperous. Large numbers of fighting men were kept there well armed; and salt, coconuts, and paddy, enough to last for several years, were stored for future use if the Tamils should attempt to take the fort.

This new city was *Jayawardhana-pura* or *Jayawardhana-kotte*, the City of Victory, now called *Kotte* or *Cotta*. Very peaceful are the occupations of its people now, but five hundred years ago it was indeed a *kottuwa* or fort, and the capital of a king.

While Kotte was still being built and fortified, Vikrama Bahu III died, and was succeeded by **Bhuvaneka Bahu V** Arya Chakra-varti, king of Jaffna, thought he might now try to bring the Sinhalese country under his rule. He came with his ships and made himself master of the nine ports belonging to the Sinhalese. Finding that he could go no farther inland, he ordered the Sinhalese to pay him a heavy tax and appointed collectors to see that the money was duly paid. Alakesvara waited at Rayigama, and when the Tamils sailed away he went on strengthening his new fort at Kotte. As soon as he was satisfied that the Sinhalese were strong enough to fight, he began to defy the Tamils. The first thing he did was to hang the tax-collectors. When Arya Chakravavarti heard of this he "kindled with rage like unto a cobra which strikes terror by its poison," and getting down thousands of men from Chola, he ordered both Gampola, the capital, and Kotte, the new city, to be attacked at the same time. One division of his army came by land and halted at Matale. This frightened king Bhuvaneka who fled from Gampola to Rayigama. His subjects, who were not terrified by the Tamils, were disgusted, for it was expected of their king that he should lead them in battle against an enemy. "What is the use," said they, "of a king who has deserted an army like ours?" They boldly entered the Tamil camp by night and slew large numbers of the enemy. The Tamils who escaped tried to get back to Jaffna but most of them lost their way among the hills and perished there.

The troops sent by Arya Chakravarti against Kotte came by sea. They landed at Panadure, and so many were they that they held all the coast from Panadure to Chilaw. The chief part of the army encamped at Gorakane in Demetagoda, where Alakesvara attacked and utterly defeated them. Then he routed the others, burnt their ships at Panadure, and returned to Rayigama.

Alakesvara was now the first man in Lanka, and honours of every kind were bestowed upon him. Poets sang his praises.

> "Mighty in cleaving the skulls of foes who are strong as elephants,
> May the Lion, the Chief of the people of Lanka, gloriously triumph."

XXXI.

THE SIXTH PARAKRAMA

When all danger from the Tamils was over, king Bhuvenaka returned to Gampola. But the people whom he had deserted would no longer have him for their king, and he found shelter in Kotte, leaving Gampola and the hill districts to be governed by a prince named Vira Bahu.

It is difficult to get any clear idea of what happened in Lanka after these events; but one or two events of importance may be noted. Not long after Bhuvenaka Bahu V. died, a Chinese general named *Ching-Ho* came to Lanka with offerings to the tooth-relic which was then kept in Kotte. It may be that he also demanded that the king of Lanka should acknowledge the emperor of China as his superior and pay tribute to China. But from some cause a quarrel arose and the Chinese general and his company were insulted and badly treated. It was with difficulty they got back to their ships. Three or four years later Ching-Ho came again with an army large enough to punish those who had injured him. Kotte was plundered and several prisoners were taken to China, among them the king or, as is more likely, a great chief who was supposed to be the king. He was afterwards sent back by the Chinese emperor who ordered that the crown of Lanka should be given to the "wisest" member of the royal family.

Then ruled a prince who is known as **Parakrama Bahu the Sixth**, and his long reign of fifty-two years is rightly considered a famous one. To begin with, he "thought it not proper that there should be two seats of government in Lanka"—that is, he did not wish to share the government of Lanka with the Tamil king of Jaffna, but decided to bring the whole island under his own rule alone, and so have one capital only.

Between the king's country and the Jaffna districts there stretched the wild jungles of the Vanni, which eighteen Tamil chiefs, calling themselves *Vanniyar*, divided among themselves: These Vanniyar obeyed neither the king of Jaffna nor the king of Lanka, for the two kings had enough to do in watching each other, and the Vanni jungles were not easy to get across. Parakrama, however, boldly led his army against the lawless Vanniyar, captured their forts, and compelled them to pay him a yearly tribute of elephants.

The king of Jaffna was not pleased to hear of the success of the Sinhalese and he defied them by publicly proclaiming himself emperor of Lanka—not as before king of Jaffna only. Parakrama took up the challenge. A prince named *Sapumal* was sent with an army against the king of Jaffna. "Tell him," said Parakrama to Sapumal, "that as it is not fit that Lanka should have two emperors, I have sent you to relieve him of that new title; and as he could not rest contented with what he had, you will give him somewhat more rest."

Sapumal was a prince of more than ordinary size and strength, and when he rode on his great black horse it seemed as if no one could resist him. The first invasion of Jaffna was not very successful, but at the second attempt Sapumal entered the city, and made its streets "run red with blood." Jaffna once again became subject to the Sinhalese king of Lanka.

On several other occasions Parakrama had to fight against the enemies of his country.

The king of Canara, a country on the Indian coast, west cf Mysore, is said to have invaded Lanka in this reign; but his attempt to conquer the island failed. Again, a Sinhalese trading ship which sailed to one of the Indian ports was seized with its cargo, and the sailors were made prisoners by the raja of that place. When news of this was brought to Parakrama he sent a number of ships, plundered and destroyed several Cholian villages, and made the raja pay him a yearly tribute. Then in Lanka itself there was trouble again. The prince who ruled the five Kandyan districts (Uda Nuwara, Yati Nuwara, Harispattu, Hewaheta, and Dumbara) thought he could be an independent king, and rebelled against Parakrama. This rebellion was put down with much bloodshed and a prince of the royal line was appointed governor of the Kandyan province. From these conquests—of the Vanni, Jaffna, Canara, Chola, and Kandy—we understand that Parakrama Bahu VI. was a warrior as much to be feared and respected as was the first Parakrama.

Buddhism flourished during this reign. The tooth-relic was carefully kept within four golden caskets, one within the other, and a splendid temple three-storeys high was built for it at Kotte. Robes and alms were given year by year to the priests. Colleges were established for their education, and the most learned among them were employed in making copies of the sacred books.

One of the priests who lived at this time

was *Sri Rahula* of Totagamuwa, a village near Galle, and him the king specially favoured. Sri Rahula was the head priest of a temple not far from Kotte, and his knowledge of six languages together with his skill in arguing on Buddhism made him famous throughout Lanka. But he was even more famous as a poet, and he is indeed regarded as the greatest of Sinhalese poets. Between him and the king there was the warmest affection, and the poet's writings are full of passages in praise of the king.

XXXII.

THE PORTUGUESE AND THE MOORS

We come now to the end of what may be called the *Sinhalese period* of the history of Lanka, and to the beginning of a long struggle which the Sinhalese carried on for three hundred years to keep themselves a free and independent nation. For two thousand years they had been rulers of Lanka, though for nearly all that time they had to fight hard against the Tamils who tried to take the country from them. The Sinhalese were now to meet a much more powerful enemy from a country very far away, a country which was not much larger than their own, but whose people were better trained for fighting both on land and on the sea, with larger ships and far more dangerous weapons of war.

This far country was *Portugal* in Europe, and its people were called the *Portuguese*. They were the finest sailors of those days, though their ships were quite small compared with the great steamers which people travel in to-day; and, of course, they knew nothing of the use of steam for driving ships. But even in those small sailing-ships of theirs they were continually trying to discover new countries in various parts of the world. This they did partly to teach people their religion—the Christian religion—but chiefly to enlarge their empire and their trade. What they specially wished was to find a way by sea to India, a land of whose riches they had heard much, and from which the people of Europe obtained the spices (such as cinnamon, pepper, and cloves) for which they were willing to pay exceedingly high prices.

The spices and other products of Asia were taken by Arab traders to Egypt, and from there European ships took them to the towns of Europe where they could be sold. The Arabs were bold sailors whose ships sailed everywhere in the Indian Ocean from Java and Borneo to Suez, and who allowed no other people to interfere with their valuable trade in the East. Lanka was a useful country for them. The harbours of Galle and Colombo were convenient places for the exchange of goods from the different countries of Asia and

Eastern Africa. From China came silk and cloves; from India, pepper, brass, and cloth; from Persia, horses; while Lanka itself provided elephants and the finest cinnamon in the world. The Arab name for Lanka was *Serendib* or *Selendib*, *(Sinha-dwipa)* which the Portuguese changed into *Ceilan*, and others after them into *Ceylon*.

When at last the Portuguese, under a captain named Vasco da Gama, succeeded in their attempt and found their way by sea into the Indian Ocean, they found the Arabs trading there, and many battles had to be fought before the power of the Arabs could be broken. The Portuguese called them *Moors* because the Arabs were Muhammadans, and *Moor* was the name generally given to the Muhammadans in Portugal and Spain.

The Portuguese went first to Calicut on the south-west of India and, though the Arabs or Moors tried hard to prevent it, they arranged a trade between Portugal and Calicut. They came again and again to India, and soon succeeded in making settlements at Goa and a few other places on the west coast. Not long afterwards they established stations in Asia as far east as Malacca.

XXXIII.

THE PORTUGUESE IN LANKA

Lanka was not unknown to the Portuguese but for some years they were too busy in India to visit the island. One day, however, the Portuguese governor of Goa heard that the Moors were still carrying on their trade between the Red Sea and Malacca, but that, to avoid the Portuguese, their ships sailed south of Lanka and close by the Maldive Islands. The governor ordered his son *Lorenzo de Almeida* to capture these ships. Lorenzo sailed from Goa, but the monsoon winds of that season prevented him from reaching the Maldives and drove him to the harbour of Colombo.

The news of his arrival was at once taken to the King **Dharma Parakrama Bahu IX.** at Kotte. "There is now in our harbour a race of people fair of skin and comely. They wear jackets of iron and hats of iron. They rest not a minute in one place; they walk here and there. They eat pieces of stone and drink blood. They give two or three pieces of gold and silver for one fish or one lime. The noise of their cannon is louder than thunder. Their cannon balls fly many a league and break to pieces fortresses of granite." Such is said to have been the report carried to the king. We may well believe that the people were surprised and even alarmed.

The principal chiefs met together to consider how the new arrivals should be treated, and one of them, Chakra-yuddha, offered to go to the harbour and see for himself how much of the news brought to the king was true. He went, not robed as a chief but in the clothes of an ordinary villager, so that without being himself noticed he might find out all that he wanted to know. As the result of his visit and of the information he took back to the king, the Portuguese were allowed to stay awhile in Colombo without being harmed. They asked to see the king and one or two of them were taken to the capital. But the Sinhalese did not wish the strangers to know how near Kotte was to the harbour, and they were therefore led through jungles so thick with trees that they could scarcely see the sun, and by paths with so many turnings to one side and another that the strangers were completely puzzled! Even now the Sinhalese have a saying, "Like the Portuguese going to Kotte," when they speak about getting to any place by a very long and winding road.

For a whole day they travelled in this manner, and at last they were brought before a chief whom they believed to be the king. The meeting took place at night, and it was agreed that the Sinhalese king should pay a certain quantity of cinnamon every year to the Portuguese who in return would protect him and his country from enemies Don Lorenzo then took into his ships the first year's payment of cinnamon and sailed back to Goa. This happened in the year 1506.

Twelve years afterwards the Portuguese came again with seventeen ships and this time they came to begin the actual conquest of Lanka. They built a fort at Colombo and little by little occupied more of the island till in time all the districts on the sea-coast were brought under their rule. They built forts at every important place, and churches too. They were Roman Catholic Christians, and they did all they could to make the Sinhalese and Tamils also Christians. Most of the Christians in Lanka to-day are Roman Catholics. We may note besides that they were the first to bring a European language to Lanka, which is still spoken here though in a corrupt form.

The Portuguese held the low-country for a hundred and thirty four years (1506-1640 A.D.) and during all that time had to fight continually against the Sinhalese kings in the hill country, who for greater safety removed the capital from Kotte to Sitavaka (Avisavella) and then to Kandy. The Sinhalese kingdom began at this time to be called the **Kandyan** kingdom, and all the Sinhalese who could not bear the rule of the Portuguese left the low-country and lived among the Kandyans. Here the Portuguese could not follow them, for it was not easy to find a way through the thick, sunless jungles and wide rivers, and steep, high mountains, which separated the hill-country from the provinces of the coast. On a few occasions the Portuguese in their wars with the Sinhalese tried to follow their enemy to the hills, but they were always beaten. At the Balane Pass near Kadugannawa more than one fierce fight ended in defeat for the Portuguese. *Constantine de Saa*, the noblest of all the Portuguese governors of the low-country, once went as far as Uva, and here he and his little army were betrayed and killed though they fought most bravely.

XXXIV.

THE V. O. C.

The Portuguese were not the only Europeans who wanted to trade with India and the other countries of the East : there were also the *Dutch* (the people of Holland) and the *English*. But the Portuguese, who had with so much difficulty found the way by sea to India, kept the secret carefully to themselves, and for some years they were the only Europeans whose ships sailed to and from India. The Dutch and the English had to buy the spices of the East from them.

Then, the Portuguese were conquered by the Spaniards (the people of Spain) and were forbidden to trade with the Dutch who were the enemies of Spain. This made the Dutch determined to send their own ships to India. The rich merchants of Holland formed a Company to trade with the East and their ships soon succeeded in sailing round the Cape of Good Hope and in reaching India. This

Company was called the *Vereenigde Oost-Indische Compagnie,* the United East-India Company, and the initials V. O. C. may still be seen on old coins and over old gateways in the low-country.

The Dutch and the Portuguese were now at war in the East, and one by one the Portuguese settlements in Asia fell into the hands of the Dutch. There were several reasons why these two nations should fight against each other. First, they were rivals in trade. Then, the Portuguese were the subjects, of the King of Spain who had cruelly oppressed the Dutch when they too were his subjects, and who sought to bring them again under his power. Again, though the Dutch and the Portuguese were both Christian nations, they nevertheless differed from each other on many important points of religion. The Portuguese were Roman Catholic Christians while most of the Dutch were *Protestant* Christians. or, as they put it, they belonged to the "True Reformed Christian Religion." But it was for trade reasons chiefly that the Dutch attacked the Portuguese wherever they could in the East.

At the end of May in the year 1602, a Dutch admiral, *Joris van Spilbergen,* came with his ships to Batticaloa, from Batavia, the head-quarters of the Dutch in Asia. He said he had come to buy pepper and cinnamon. The people of Batticaloa, who knew very little about Europe or the Europeans, thought he was a Portuguese, and were greatly surprised to find that he belonged to a different nation and to a nation which was unfriendly to the Portuguese. Spilbergen heard that there was a king of Kandy. He went to Kandy and was well received when the king (**Vimala Dharma I.**) found out that the Dutch would help him against the Portuguese. An agreement was made by which the Dutch were allowed to trade freely with the Sinhalese if they would drive the Portuguese out of Lanka.

It was not, however, till the year 1640, when **Raja Sinha II**. was king of Kandy. that the Dutch came over to conquer Lanka. In that year Galle and other towns were taken from the Portuguese and a sort of government was established. In a few years the Portuguese were driven out and all the sea-coast provinces came under new rulers.

The Dutch did not trouble themselves about the hill country governed by Raja Sinha II. They had enough to do in the low-country and their chief enemies were the Moors who interfered with the trade, and the Portuguese whom they regarded as spies. With the king of Kandy the Dutch tried to live at peace, but naturally there were continual quarrels.

In the low-country the Dutch ruled less harshly than the Portuguese and did much for the good of the people. They opened schools in plenty for both boys and girls, and insisted upon the children being taught. They established courts of law where justice was done without favour to the rich or the great, and though some of their laws were harsh towards Moors, Portuguese, and those who were not

Protestant Christians, most of their laws had the effect of improving the habits of the people. They helped agriculture in every way and tried to introduce new plants such as tea, cocoa, and wheat, into the island. Like the old kings of Lanka they took great pains to build and repair tanks and canals. But they made a mistake in forcing the Sinhalese and Tamils to become Christians.

It was during early Dutch times that an Englishman named *Robert Knox* came to Kottiyar, near Trincomalie, and was taken prisoner with his companions by the Kandyans. Knox lived in the Kandyan districts for twenty years and then he managed to escape to Arippu. He afterwards got back to England. He wrote a book about his imprisonment and it gives us valuable information about the Kandyan kingdom of those times.

XXXV.

THE ENGLISH IN LANKA.

The English were as eager to get to India as the other peoples of Europe, and English merchants formed an East India Company about the same time as the Dutch. The Dutch and the English fought frequently against each other in various parts of Asia, and when Holland was forced to take part in the great wars which the nations of Europe fought in those days, her navy suffered, and she lost much of her power. Many of her possessions thus fell into the hands of the English and the coast provinces of Lanka became English territory in the year 1796. They were ruled by the English *East India Company* and were at first under the Company's governor of Madras. But this arrangement did not turn out well, and two years later Lanka was made a Crown Colony: that is, it was ruled by a Governor who was sent direct from England, and who was responsible not to the Company but to the king of England.

It was not till 1815 that the English got possession of the Kandyan kingdom. In the previous year *Ehelapola*, the principal Kandyan chief, fled to Colombo from Kandy complaining of the Kandyan king's bad government. The king **Sri Vikrama Raja Sinha**, a Tamil, was reported to be a cruel ruler and his subjects were said to be anxious to get rid of him. He punished Ehelapola by murdering that chief's wife and children in a savage fashion. He then began to ill-treat people who were under British rule. The English governor, Sir Robert Brownrigg, decided to send an army against Kandy.

Ehelapola guided the British troops, who entered the capital with scarcely any fighting. The king was taken prisoner, declared to be no longer king, and sent to Vellore in South India. Lanka—or Ceylon, as we may now call our island—was declared to be a British possession.

Now for the first time was the whole island under the rule of a European power.

There were two or three risings or "rebellions" against the British, but after 1848 the people settled down contentedly under British rule. As the country became quieter and better accustomed to English ideas and customs they obtained more and more liberty. The laws made by the Dutch against the Roman Catholics and the Moors were gradually taken away. Nobody was forced to become a Christian, and Buddhists were specially protected. Schools were re-opened, and natives of Ceylon were promoted to high positions in the government. One of the most important benefits to the country was the opening of a good road from Colombo to Kandy—a work that took ten years to finish.

The hill districts were found suitable for growing coffee, and soon large "estates" of coffee covered the hillsides. After about fifty years a disease attacked the coffee trees, the crops failed. and many people were ruined. The European planters then turned to tea, cocoa, cinchona, and other products. The people of the country went on growing rice and coconuts.

The sale of these products made the island rich and enabled roads to be opened in places where formerly people were afraid to live. These were not enough, and railways were made by which goods and people are more easily and quickly carried from place to place. Steamers came in greater numbers to take away goods and bring other goods in their place. A larger harbour became necessary. Galle was the chief port of Lanka, but it was thought that Colombo would be more useful, and a splendid harbour was made there. The result is that Colombo is now one of the largest and most important towns in the East,

XXXVI.

THE LANKA OF TO-DAY

We have now come to the end of our present study of the History of Ceylon, and it will be of some use to us to know how the island is governed at the present time. There are over four millions of people in Ceylon, and of these two and a quarter millions are Sinhalese and about a million are Tamils; but more than 350,000 of the Tamils are labourers from India who work in the planting districts. There are, in fact, more Indian Tamils in Ceylon than Ceylon Tamils. Besides these races there are others—English, Burghers, Malays, Moors, Veddas, and so on. Generally speaking, the Sinhalese are Buddhists, the Tamils are Hindus, the Europeans and their descendants are Christians, the Malays and Moors are Muhammadans.

One of the first things we have to learn is that all of us must live in peace and friendliness with one another, and must all work together not only for our own good but also for the good of the whole country. It is worse than foolish for one race to abuse or to act against another, since we can get on only by helping one another. Each of us can be proud of his own race and at the same time respect others and be courteous to them.

We live under English or British rule and belong to what is known as the British Empire, the largest of all the empires now ruling in the world. Our Ceylon is only a very small portion of the vast dominions of the king of England. If a page of this book represents Ceylon more than four hundred and fifty such pages would be required to shew the size of the British Empire!

The king of England is also king of Ceylon, and he sends *Governors* here to rule the country for him. A Governor's term of office is usually five or six years.

To help the Governor in deciding what should be done for the good of the island there are two Councils. One is the **Executive Council**, whose business it is to see that the laws are carried out. It is now composed of some of the highest officers of Government with three members who are not officers of Government. The other is the **Legislative Council**; that is, the law-making council. Its business is to say what laws should be made, and how the money of the Government should be spent. But the king of England decides in the end on every important matter.

Important changes have been made lately in the Legislative Council. The Council is now made up of fourteen *official* and twenty-three *unofficial* members. The official members are those who hold office under the Government. The unofficials are persons who are not connected with the Government; their duty is to speak for the people in the island, saying what the people want and what they think about the doings of the Government.

The twenty-three unofficials are made up in this way; sixteen are *elected*, or chosen, by the people,—eleven by the nine provinces (the Western Province electing three instead of one), two by the Europeans, and one each by the Burghers, the Ceylon Chamber of Commerce, and the Low-country Products Association. Seven unofficials are *nominated*, that is, named or appointed, by the Governor,—two for the Kandyans, one each for the Muhammadans and the Indians in Ceylon; and three others as the Governor sees fit and necessary. It will not be long before the Kandyan, Muhammadan, and Indian members are elected instead of nominated.

The most important change is that there are now more unofficial members than official members, so that very great power and responsibility are placed in the hands of the people of the country. But it is the Government, after all, which is responsible for safety and order in the island, and therefore the Governor has the power to pass any law which he thinks is quite necessary, and to prevent the passing of any law which he thinks undesirable. But this is a power which he will rarely need to use.

The laws of Ceylon are called **Ordinances**. Members of the Executive and Legislative Councils are given the title of *Honourable* so long as they are members of either Council.

Next to the Governor is the **Colonial Secretary**. He is the Governor's chief assistant and adviser. When the Governor is away from the island the Colonial Secretary takes his place and becomes the Acting Governor. The Colonial Secretary is the highest member in rank of the **Ceylon Civil Service**, which consists of a number of Government officers appointed on the results of an examination held in England. A few are appointed in Ceylon to the *Local Division* of this Service.

The island is divided into nine Provinces over each of which is a **Government Agent**. His office is called a *Kachcheri*. His duty is to superintend the collection of all money due to Government from his province, to settle disputes about it, to encourage agriculture, and generally to act as the head of the province.

How is money found to pay Government servants and for making roads, railways, public buildings &c.? The money is got partly by taxes, such as the poll-tax or road tax; by charges called *duties* on goods brought into the island; by the sale of licenses for arrack &c.; by the sale of *Crown lands,* or lands belonging to the Government; by the sale of postage and revenue stamps; by the fees paid by ships which come to Colombo and our other ports; by the profits of the railway. There are other ways in which money is obtained, but these are the chief. The total amount of money thus obtained is called the *Revenue* of the island.

It is the duty of all citizens to obey the laws of the land, for if the laws are not obeyed, there can be no order or quiet for any of us. When people disobey the laws they are brought before the Judges of our Courts of Law. So also where two parties have disputes about property or money, or when one person injures another, the Courts decide between them. The highest court in the island is called the **Supreme Court**, where all the most important matters are decided. Next come the **District Courts**, and next to these the **Police Courts**, where the smallest offences against the law are heard. When small sums of money are in dispute, the cases are heard by **Courts of Requests**. In many places there are village courts called **Gansabhawas**.

We have good reason to be thankful for the benefits we enjoy under British rule. It is very doubtful, to say the least, if under the rule of any other nation we should be so well off. We are so used to the peace and the freedom we have that we do not think sufficiently of their value. So long as we do not disobey the law, or annoy other people, we can do almost anything we choose to do. Any man can take up whatever occupation he likes, or enter any profession for which he can fit himself. He can go wherever he pleases and say whatever he pleases. He can rise to almost any position, whatever his race or caste or religion. For his convenience there are roads, railways, steamers, post offices, telegraphs, telephones, schools, hospitals. He has rights which he can use, and privileges which he can enjoy. But every right and every privilege has a duty attached to it, and it is most important that we should remember our duties. Every bad citizen is a hindrance to the advancement of his country. The more good citizens there are, the sooner will our rights and privileges be extended.

LIST OF TERMS

Bali offerings (p. 51)—offerings made to demons, etc. to gain their favour or turn away their anger.

Crown Colony (p. 127)—a country governed directly by the King's officers, *e.g.* Ceylon, Mauritius the West Indies. Colonies like South Africa, Canada, and Australia used to be known as *self-governing* Colonies and are now styled the *Dominions*. From its size and importance Ceylon is often spoken of as the *Premier*, or the first, Crown Colony.

Dagaba (also called **thupa** and **cetiya**)—a bell shaped building meant originally to enclose a relic of Buddha.

Durbar or **darbar** (p. 105)—a court or public reception held by a prince.

Prabhu-raja (p. 111)—a Viceroy or sub-King.

Revenue (p. 133)—the annual income of a government from taxation, etc.; public expenses are paid from the revenue.

Vihara—a dwelling-place for priests; usually near a dagaba.

INDEX